Matriliny in Meghalaya
Tradition and Change

– Editor –

Pariyaram M. Chacko

2022

Regency Publications

A Division of

Astral International Pvt. Ltd.

New Delhi - 110 002

First Published, 1998
Reprinted, 2022

ISBN: 978-81-86030-69-1 (Hardbound)

Published by : **Regency Publications**
A Division of
Astral International Pvt. Ltd.
– ISO 9001:2015 Certified Company –
4736/23, Ansari Road Darya
Ganj, New Delhi - 110 002 Phone:
011-4354 9197, 2327 8134 Fax:
+91-11-2324 3060
E-mail: info@astralint.com
Website: www.astralint.com

Printed at : **Replika Press Pvt Ltd**

To
Shonu

Foreword

India is veritably a unity in diversity. It is an amazing phenomenon that different ethnic, linguistic and religious groups exist therein with their own varied cultural subsystems. This great Indian diversity can be discovered and appreciated if only adequate attention is paid to the study of frontier communities. Marriage and family practices exhibit a wide variety of patterns. Matriliny has existed in South as well as in North-East India. Though it has almost disappeared from the Hindu community of Nairs in Kerala, it is still cherished and followed among the Muslim Islanders of Lakshadweep and among the tribal, both Christian and non-Christian, inhabitants of the hill State of Meghalaya.

It gives me great pleasure that Dr. Pariyaram M. Chacko has brought out this timely volume on the changing trends of the matrilineal system of Meghalaya. It is quite gratifying to note that most of the papers are contributed by scholars who themselves are from within the matrilineal system. Their own experiences, observations and perspectives carry a special authenticity and convey to the readers the insiders' view of tradition and change in their own society. I have no doubt that this book is a valuable contribution to the literature on the emerging family trends in North-East India.

Prof. Barrister Pakem
Vice-Chancellor
North-Eastern Hill University
Shillong, Meghalaya

Acknowledgements

I wish to thank all the authors for their contributions. All these papers except one were read during a one-day seminar which was organised with a financial grant from the Indian Council of Social Science Research, North-Eastern Regional Centre. Thanks are due to ICSSR-NERC for its support. I am indebted to Mr. P.S. Thomas and Mr. Godfrey Pathaw for their secretarial assistance.

Shillong **Pariyaram M. Chacko**

Contents

Contributors

Aldila Mawlong is doing her Ph.D. in the Department of Sociology, North-Eastern Hill University, Shillong.

Dominic Jala SDB is Provincial of the Salesian Province at Gauhati.

Frederick S. Downs is Professor of History at the United Theological College, Bangalore.

I.M. Syiem teaches Sociology at St. Edmund's College, Shillong.

Juanita War is Professor, Department of Linguistics, North-Eastern Hill University, Shillong.

O.L. Snaitang is Professor of History at Serampore Theological College.

Pariyaram M. Chacko is Reader, Department of Sociology, North-Eastern Hill University, Shillong.

Philomath Passah is Professor, Department of Economics, North-Eastern Hill University, Shillong.

Sohblei Sngi Lyngdoh is an indigenous and activist missionary. He teaches Theology at Sacred Heart Theological College, Shillong.

1

Introduction

Pariyaram M. Chacko

Meghalaya, a small hill state in the north-eastern part of India is the abode of three matrilineal tribes, namely the Khasis, the Jaintias and the Garos. The first two tribes are very similar to each other and both use Khasi as written language though the Jaintias have their own dialect. According to the 1991 census there are 1,760,626 people in Meghalaya. The Khasi region of the state has 8,74,622 people, the Jaintia hills have a population of 2,19,186 and the Garo region has a population of 6,66,818. About 81 per cent of the population in Meghalaya consists of the tribals. The state is mostly spread on a mountainous region. Most of the indigenous people are engaged in agriculture. Shifting cultivation is still common. However a sizable population have taken up modern professions, a large number being employed in Government and semi-Government institutions. Many are found in trade and business concerns.

Before the Britishers established their supremacy in the early nineteenth century, the region relatively remained isolated. The British annexed Khasi Hills in 1833 and the Jaintia Hills in 1835. The Christian missionaries arrived in 1841. These events opened up the region to the outside world. Some non-tribals came to work in different capacities. The modern system of administration along with its legal framework came into the midst of the tribals. The traditional economy was greatly disturbed by the introduction of monetary and market economy. The introduction and expansion of road and other communication channels was breaking down the age-old isolation of the hill tribes. The Christian missionaries introduced the Roman script and transformed the Khasi and the Garo dialects into written languages. The missionary effort popularised education. Shillong, the state capital, is known throughout the north-eastern region of India as a centre of education. A good standard of health care and hygiene also was set. Many tribals became Christians. As per the 1991 census of India, 64 per cent of Meghalaya people are Christians. Since 1971 Meghalaya is a full-fledged state within India with all its benefits and responsibilities. Its government is run by the tribals themselves. Today the people of Meghalaya are no longer isolated.

The Matrilineal Units of the Khasis

The largest matrilineal unit of the Khasis is the *Kur* (clan). The members of a clan believed themselves descended from an ancestor, Ka *Iawbei Tynrai*. Genealogical relationship between clan members cannot be traced. The *kur* are strictly exogamous and any inter-marriage between its members is considered the worst sin a Khasi can commit. Each clan has its own cromlech (*Mawbah*) where the bones of their members are interned. Besides, each clan has its common land and a council. Those members of a clan who live in one domestic unit or in different domestic units in the same neighbourhood constitute a lineage or *Kpoh*. Attendance of all members of a *kpoh* is the norm for common functions like marriage and death.

All the descendants of a grand-mother along with the youngest daughter (*Khadduh*) and the ancestral house usually constitutes *Iing*, family. Children address their mother's sisters and female maternal cousins as mothers. Their spouses are classificatory fathers. The eldest living brother (*Kni*) exercises authority in all matters. The household unit of a mother, her husband and children is also called *Iing*. While the *Khadduh's* husband is expected to reside with her, all other sisters settle nearby in their own independent households with their husbands and children. Thus fission of an *Iing* is a frequent feature unlike the *tharavad* of the Nairs of South

India. In such independent households, the authority of the *Kni* is not as pervasive as in his natal *Iing*. Though most of the wealth is inherited by *Khadduh*, she is only a custodian. It is the *Kni* who manages the property on her behalf. Traditionally, the *Khadduh* had the financial responsibility of looking after the welfare of all the *Iing* members and of ensuring proper religious rites at the appropriate occasions. However, *Kni* carried out these tasks on her behalf and he was also the priest and chief celebrant in all rituals as there was no separate institution of priesthood nor any institutionalised religion. In contrast to the *Kni*, the husband of the *Khadduh* had no great role to play except that of procreation. If he wanted to exercise any power, he could do so as *Kni* in his own natal *Iing*. In traditional times, the marriages were arranged by the *Kni* who himself blessed them in a simple ceremony at the bride's residence. There was no dowry nor bride price. The marriage was monogamous though divorce and remarriage were permitted.

Though *Kur* and *Kpoh* still exist their hold over the people has been on the wane. The authority and sanctity of *Kni* have come under pressure. He does not wield much power in conducting his sister's household affairs. Many *Khadduhs* exercise proprietary rights over landed property. A large number of Khasi men and women have taken up modern professions and have fixed income. They seem to set up nuclear households along with their husbands. Christianity has introduced a set of values regarding family and marriage like the sanctity of the marriage, the importance of a father, and avoidance of pre-marital and extra-marital sex. The assimilation of these values has given rise to giving more importance to a child's father than to his mother's brother. The institution of the *Khadduh* is closely associated with the traditional religion. Since the spread of Christianity, the *Khadduh* no longer plays the role of a custodian of the religion, its rites and its *Mawbah*. *Kni's* function as a priest has also vanished.

There are many surmises and opinions expressed by various authors about the Khasi matriliny and the changes that have taken place therein. However very few research works based on fieldwork are available on the subject. Nakane's[1] study is an excellent one based on field data. Many authors assert that the lion's share of the property goes to the *Khadduh*. However no one is sure how much is this lion's share ? What is the exact share given to each sister of an *Iing* ? Besides property issues, we have also no real data on marriage stability. We also need to know more exactly the gains the husbands have made in the changed circumstances. Have they come to play more authoritative role in his wife's *Iing* ? In a remarkable paper, Nongbri asserts that "the Khasi matrilineal system does not actually favour women although certain aspects of their ideology and inheritance rules may give a contrary impression."[2] Moreover, "The rights and privileges of women in Khasi matriliny turn out to be mere burdensome duties and responsibilities."[3] According to Nongbri, the male bias is reflected in the Meghalaya Succession to Self Acquired Property Act 1984. The subordination of women is seen in their exclusion from the *durbars* and other political wings. According to her the attempt made by some organisations to project matrilineal descent as detrimental to economic interest is a dangerous portend as it will further reduce the importance of the Khasi women.[4] In the light of the differing perceptions of the Khasi matriliny, there is a need for more quantitative and qualitative data. The writings of the scholars who themselves are from the matrilineal community will constitute rich materials for new insights and perspectives. In this aspect this volume will be a welcome addition to the literature on matriliny.

Pariyaram M. Chacko in his paper on *Matrilineal System: Some Structural Implications* aims at apprising the readers about some structural characteristics of the matriliny compared to patriliny. Since descent is traced through female and authority is vested with the male matrikin, there is an immense difference in matriliny. The structural prerequisites of maintaining the systems require that the status of the father is downgraded, father-children relationship is underplayed and the stability of the marriage is not emphasized. All these notions are contrary to patrilineal values. Therefore, some patrilineal people view the matrilineal system with some bias little knowing that matriliny is not merely tracing descent through female sex, but is loaded with certain values regarding marriage fatherhood, and motherhood.

Juanita War delves deep into the various units of the family among the Khasis and the Jaintias in her paper on *The Khasi Concept of Family: Changes in Structure and Functions.* Although *Ka iing tnat* is the smallest household unit, for all practical purposes *ka Iing* is the effective family unit. After discussing various matrilineal units like, *Iing, Kpoh* and *Kur,* their functions are discussed in detail. As in all matrilineal societies, so too in Khasi society there are several sets of conflict situations. Some of these are: conflicts between nuclear family and matrilineal descent groups; the conflict between natal and conjugal loyalties; the conflict between ownership of the property and authority, and the conflict between a man's children and his sister's children. Education, urbanisation, employment opportunities in non-agricultural sectors and change from subsistence economy to market economy have undermined the traditional matrilineal structures. As a result of these, increasing importance is being given to elementary families (husband-wife units). The *Iing,* the *Kpoh* and the *Kur* are no longer strong forces of social cohesion and solidarity as they were in the past.

Sohblei Sngi Lyngdoh is an indigenous missionary with a lot of pastoral experience. His paper entitled, *The Khasi Matriliny: Its Past and its Future* is the outcome of his own experience and observation. His emotional involvement with his own people is reflected in his earnest concern for the welfare of his society. He believes that in the original matrilineal system of the Khasis, the *Kni* played the crucial role. He was the centre of the authority and the economy. He was the pivot around which his sisters and their children revolved. The father of the children was merely a genitor with no important role to play in his wife's family. The uncle's authority was so powerful that he could punish severely recalcitrant nephews and neices. He was the chief administrator of all goods, movable and immovable, which were principally earned by him. He was also the priest, the teacher and the intermediary between God and his sister's children. He acted also as a medicine man. Even before the Britishers arrived the system had undergone change, because the Khasis discarded the following simple law: in every village there should be more or less an equal number of congnate and agnate families (*Ki*

Kur and *Kikha*) so that they can easily find marriage partners within the village. When spouses had to be sought in distant villages, the traditional system could not survive and the husbands were forced to stay with their wives. The *Kni* slowly disappeared from his sister's house. Sngi Lyngdoh thinks that the disintegration of the ancient matriliny started much before the Britishers or the Christian missionaries arrived. However the Britishers contributed to the decline of the uncle's authority, by recognising the *Khadduh* as the heiress. Christianity as such has not brought about any change. It did not interfere with the system. The Khasi society is going through a difficult period because though the uncle has lost his pivotal role, the father has not yet attained his due role. There is an authority vacuum. There is no one to bring up the children in proper discipline. The father is still an outsider. The need of the hour for the Khasis is to stop this drift.

The subject of discussion, in I.M. Syiem's paper, *Religion and Matriliny in Khasi Society: Some Observations*, is the relationship between religion and matriliny. The Khasi religion is not an organised one and it functions at the family and at the clan level. It is inextricably bound up with the matrilineal practices. The eldest uncle is the spiritual mediator and the *Khadduh* is the keeper of the religion. The *Kni* invokes both God and Grandmother who are equally responsible for the well-being of the clan. The Khasi religion, *Ka niam* is vital for the preservation of the matriliny. Since Christianity has replaced the traditional religion, the matrilineal system is bound to change in some ways. However many converted Christians have not internalized the Christian values and many are influenced by the local practices. Many of them still consult the traditional diviners to find out the causes of their misfortunes. Abandoning the traditional faith while retaining matriliny does not seem to be an easy task. The most vital challenge to the system has not come from Christianity, but from within the Khasi society itself. Property ownership has become a pivotal issue. The younger generations are questioning the trusteeship of the *Khadduh* and demanding a share for themselves, particularly for the sons.

O.L. Snaitang, an indigenous theologian exposes a novel idea that Christianity did not destabilise the matrilineal system, but actually contributed to its strengthening. With increasing exposure to the British rule and the patrilineal cultures all around, the Khasi matriliny, would have crumbled but for the support of the churches. The church helped modify the system to survive. By disallowing frequent divorces and polygamy on the part of men, the marriage system was stabilised. By popularising education and health care, the church strengthened the capacity of the people to successfully adjust to a modern world. O.L. Snaitang's theory is true in a short term span; but the structural implications of the stability of the marriage and the increasing responsibility of the male parenthood are that they would militate against the system in the long run. The paper *The Impact of Christianity in the Khasi-Jaintia Family* also traces the possible origin of the matriliny among the Khasis. One can see some similarity between them and the Nairs of Kerala. The Khasi-Jaintia men were hunters and raiders who rarely settled down in a home. The Nair men were mostly soldiers who spent most of their time away from home. Matriliny was a suitable arrangement in such a scenario. Snaitang believes that only theoretically the women enjoyed status, while they were almost like bonded labourers.

Philomath Passah in his short article recounts the traditional as well as the changing roles of the youngest daughter and of the maternal uncle among the Khasis and the Jaintias. The custodial right of the property in the hands of the youngest daughters have now become an absolute right. Husbands slowly replace the functions of the maternal uncles in the care of children and in the decision making process. Khasi associations like *Ka Seny Iktiar Longbriew Manbriew and Syngkong Rympei Thymmai* have made attempts to change the traditional inheritance laws in favour of the males. The Meghalaya succession to self-acquired property (Khasi and Jaintia Special Provision) Act 1984, empowering the parents to bequeath their self-acquired property has not been implemented.

Aldila Mawlong's paper *Some Aspects of Change in the Family System of the Khasis,* is the only one which presents the result of a field-survey. The study was conducted in 1995 in the city of Shillong. This paper is based on her M.Phil dissertation submitted to the North-Eastern Hill University.[5]

She interviewed 80 married individuals equally divided between men and women. Ninety per cent of the men and eighty per cent of the women were of the opinion that the husbands should be the head of the household; so too the majority think that the role of the *Kni* is now more symbolic than decisive. Ninetyfive per cent of the women and sixty-two per cent of the men think that the property should be equally divided to all sons and daughters. These results make it abundantly clear whither the winds of change are blowing. The matrilineal system has undoubtedly weakened. Equal opportunities for all children are demanded. The conjugal family ties are getting stronger at the expense of other kinship ties. However, the matrilineal descent principle is sustained, because many Khasis think that their culture is bound up with matriliny.

Dominic Jala in his brief paper, *Christian Values Encounter Family in Meghalaya* enunciates some of the Christian values on marriage and family. Many changes have occurred in Meghalaya families due to education, health care and to new occupational avenues. Christianity as such has never attempted to destroy the matrilineal culture. However, the Church is clear that marriage is a sacred bond which is not to be lightly treated. The stability of marriage is the foundation of good family life.

Status of Garo Women in the Nineteenth Century is the only one in this volume about the Garos. Frederick S. Downs, an historian, discusses the status of women in the Garo tribe by evaluating two written sources of the nineteenth century. One was a letter written by a Garo association to the Baptist missionaries in 1897. This letter while acknowledging that "the woman is the master of the riches of the house," castigates them for their evil ways; for they despised their husbands and taught evil to their daughters. The letter thanks the missionaries for their help in making them behave well. The other source was a paper by Miriam Russell, a lady missionary, which was presented in a Baptist Missionary Conference at Nagaon in 1886. According to her "the women are not honored by the men but are really held in contempt by them . . . the word of the man is the law that governs her actions." As an historian, Frederick S. Downs evaluates both these sources in terms of their authorship and purpose. It is concluded that Russel's paper is a more credible source regarding the status of Garo women. This is corroborated by some later anthropological literature. The traditional Garo society was matrilineal with strong patriarchal values.

NOTES AND REFERENCES

1. Nankane, Chie, Garo and Khasi, *A Comparative Study in Matrilineal Systems,* Paris. Monton and Company, 1967.
2. Nongbri, Tiplut, "Gender and the Khasi Family Structure: Some Implications of the Meghalaya Succession to Self-Acquired Property Act 1984", *Sociological Bulletin,* 37 (1 & 2) 1988, p. 79.
3. Ibid. p. 76.
4. Nongbri Tiplut, "Tribal Women and the Family in the Context of Meghalaya", Paper presented in Seminar on Changing Aspects of Family in Meghalaya, Dept. of Sociology, North-Eastern Hill University, Shillong, March 1988.
5. Mawlong, Aldila, Aspects of Change in the Family system Among the Khasis, M.Phil. dissertation, Department of Sociology, North Eastern Hill University, Shillong, 1996.

2

Matrilineal System: Some Structural Implications

Pariyaram M. Chacko

Though scholars may present a dispassionate and unbiased view of the matrilineal system, the same cannot be said about the majority of the patrilineal people who come in contact with the matrilineal population. They tend to believe that the matrilineal system is inferior to that of patriliny. They look down upon particularly their sexual, marital and family customs and practices. The superior attitude of the patrilineal people arises out of incorrect understanding of matriliny and also out of their own psychological and social disposition towards patrilineal system where they have been born and nurtured.

In Meghalaya and also in Lakshadweep Islands, the majority of the people still actively follow matriliny. The Khasis, the Jaintias and the Garos practise matriliny with some variations. Though the Nair Community of Kerala has been by far the most famous matrilineal people of India among the anthropological and sociological literature, scholars seem to have lost interest in them because of the disappearance of matriliny from amongst them.

The Features of Matrilineal System

According to a theory the early human society lived in promiscuity. Because of the biological factors of pregnancy and childbirth, it was easier to trace biological relationship of children to their mothers, than to their fathers. Hence human organisation at a later stage revolved around mothers than around fathers. From matriliny, there evolved patriliny when men were able to assert their superiority. This evolutionary theory from promiscuity to patriliny via matriliny is now discarded. Both patrilineal and matrilineal systems have developed and flourished independently.

By far one of the most impressive theoretical analyses about the comparative characteristics of the matrilineal and the patrilineal systems is found in the book *Matrilineal Kinship* edited by David M. Schneider and K. Gough.[1] The following features of the matrilineal principles are discussed by Schneider. According to him, both patriliny and matriliny have three characteristics in common.[2] They are: (i) In both, unilineal descent groups are exogamous (ii) Women have primary responsibility for the care of children (iii) Men have authority over women and children. However in patrilineal systems, the male sex is used as the criterion for the descent membership while in matrilineal system the principle of affiliation is the female sex. Though it may look very simple at first, there is a world of difference between the two systems.

The critical difference between the two systems is that while both the principle of group membership and the line of authority run through the male line in patrilineal societies, they are separated, between males and females in matrilineal systems, that is, while the principle of group membership runs through the female sex, the line of authority goes through the male sex. This crucial difference makes matriliny a complex institution, more complex than that of patriliny. The most important corollary that follows is that in patrilineal descent groups, women when being married are completely transferred to their affinal group, while in matrilineal descent groups married men are not completely transferred to their affinal group and they retain their membership and authority in their natal groups. "Matrilineal descent groups depend for their continuity and operation on retaining control over both male and female members."[3] In patriliny, the women are completely assimilated into the group where they are married and they are not needed by their own natal descent groups for their continuity.

In all matrilineal societies, the male members when marrying can have only limited options.[4] They can get assimilated into their wives' groups. However, they will be stiffly resisted by the male members of their wives' groups. A constant conflict will be the end-result of this attempt at assimilation into the wives' groups. The second option is that the married men can exercise complete control over their children and wives and wean them away from their matrilineal groups. In this case, the matrilineal system will break down and patriliny will inevitably arise. The third way is that they "live in peace" in their wives' groups. The structural constraint is that an in-marrying male affine cannot be given authoritative role in the group. A male should exercise that role in his own matrilineal group. A matrilineal system can survive and flourish, if only the males are completely dependent on their own natal matrilineal descent groups except for the minimal necessity of marriage. The moment they are alienated from their group, and either join wives' group or set up independent households, it will sound the death-knell of the system. Matriliny requires an "interdependence of brother and sister."[5] The sister depends on her brother for protection and authority functions, while the brother needs her and her offspring for the continuity of his own natal descent line.

The statuses of mother and wife are meticulously sustained in patrilineal societies. In contrast the statuses of father and husband are dispensable in matrilineal systems, though men are required as genitors. Sometimes even the recognition of a father can be conveniently ignored as reflected in the saying about the Nairs "No Nair knows his father". According to Schneider: "the institutionalization of very strong, lasting or intense solidartties between husband and wife is not compatible with the maintenance of matrilineal descent groups."[6] There is an in-built conflict between marital bond and the bond of descent both for the husband and the wife. The system demands priority for the descent even at the expense of close husband-wife relationship. Strong and intense affection and loyalty are required between mother and her children; equally strong affectionate bond between father and her children are discouraged. Deep emotional attachment between father and his children will lead to strain and conflict in the mother's descent groups. So too, lasting economic co-operation between a father and his child must be discouraged lest it should threaten the system. A firm link between fathers and their sons will break their matrilineal groups. The system demands that the father let go their hold over his own sons so that they become successors of their mothers' brothers and the father accepts his own sisters' sons as his own successors. From patrilineal point of view it is an unenviable task. The matrilineal system requires that a man or a woman constantly balances his or her conjugal interest with the interests of his or her descent group. Ultimately the welfare of the descent is more important, otherwise, the system cannot survive. About the Nairs, Kathleen Gough writes "In all possible respects, efforts seem to have been made to reduce the intensity of marital ties for the sake of the unity of taravad, village and kingdom. Good men were men who devoted themselves first to the service of their feudal lords and second to the welfare of their taravad. Weak and immoral men were men who became inveigled by their wives and their children, so that they tried to make unnecessary gifts to their wives and neglected their taravad."[7]

All these structural features are found among the Khasi, Jaintia and Garo systems of matriliny. If we find, that marriages are unstable or husband-wife and father-child relationships are weak in these societies as compared with patrilineal ones, it is not that the persons concerned consciously and deliberately plan them so. Nor can it be attributed to purely personal failures. These are the structural constraints. Moreover, people from the patrilineal societies have their own conceptual biases. For example, the notions of marriage and family as they are understood or practised by the patrilineal people do not have universal validity. Different societies have different systems of marriage and family. Some of the weaknesses of the matrilineal system as viewed from patrilineal point of view, turn out to be its strengths so that the system can survive. If scholars analyse the patrilineal system from a matrilineal perspective, structural weaknesses of the system can be enumerated such as subjugation of women, denial of liberty and of property rights to them and so on.

Nakane, a Japanese anthropologist who studied the Khasi-Garo system in 1950s, notes that the divorces are quite common among the Khasis, particularly divorce rate among the *Khaddubs* is greater than among the other daughters.[8] Here again, there is a definitional problem. The divorce among the matrilineal societies does not have the same validity and significance as in the patrilineal societies. Once there was intense debate among the sociologists and the anthropologists, whether the *Sambandham* among the Nairs whereby a woman could accept as many as a dozen visiting husbands could be termed as a marriage. For patrilineal people, *Sambandham* was highly unstable, and the divorce rate was very high as many husbands stopped visiting their wives. Such notions do not seem to take note of the fact that in matrilineal system, the descent stability, and its perpetuation are more important than marital stability, conjugal relationship, incidence of divorces, desertion of wives or husbands, filial bond between the father and his son and so on. The ordinary definitions of all these concepts are inapplicable in a matrilineal environment.

Some Khasis themselves have started writing about the low status of man among them, and about the unscrupulous daughters who exploit the system either alone or in connivance with the outsiders. Some of them do feel that the system of inheritance is detrimental to the full development of the sons and also to the economic development of the Meghalaya.[9] Vitiation in the system or the exploitation of the system does not necessarily mean that matriliny is undesirable or there should be a change to patriliny.

REFERENCES

1. Schneider, David, M. and Kathleen Gough (eds.), *Matrilineal Kinship*, Univ. of California Press, California, 1961.
2. "The Distinctive Features of Matrilineal Descent Groups" in David Schneider and Kathleen Gough. op. cit., p. 5.
3. Ibid. p. 8.
4. Ibid. p. 9. According to Schneider, these options are for those males who may not have any authoritative role (such as younger brothers) to play in their own descent groups.

5. Ibid. p. 11.
6. Ibid. p. 16.
7. "Nayar: Central Kerala" in David Schneider and Kathleen Gough, op. cit, pp. 360–361.
8. Nakane, Chie, *Garo and Khasi: A Comparative Study in Matrilineal system.* Mouton & Co. The Hague, Paris, 1967 p. 133.
9. See Badwar, Magdalene, "Some Institutional Factors Retarding Economic Progress Among the Khasi Community" (Memeo), Paper presented in a Seminar in NEHU, 1987.
   Pynshai Bor Syiemlieh, *The Khasis and their Matrilineal System'*, Shillong, 1994.

3

The Khasi Concept of Family: Changes in Structure and Function

Juanita War

Introduction

The Khasi — Pnar people, also known as *Ki Hynniewtrep-Hynniewskum*, have lived in the Khasi-Jaintia Hills from time immemorial.[1] They were more or less isolated within their own 'shnong' (villages), and surrounding areas that could be reached within a few day's journey. *Ka ri ki laiphew syiem* (the land of the thirty kings chiefs) also known as *ka ri u Hynniewtrep* (the land of *Hynniewstrep*), consisted of densely forested hills inaccessible to the "*mynder*" (outsider). Contacts with the outside world were usually through raids into the plains of Assam or Sylhet, and through occasional trading during market days.

The British initially entered the hills in the early Nineteenth century to negotiate for trade routes between Kamrup and Sylhet. Within a short span of time, they conquered the whole of the Khasi hills, setting up headquarters first in Mairang, then in Shillong. They brought with them a new system of administration within the British Raj, along with government institutions and machineries. They introduced advanced transport and communication system, sanatoria, hospitals, and all other infrastructures of a modern society. Along with these, they introduced an international language into hitherto monolingual society. The Welsh Missionaries brought

Christianity, a writing system through the Roman script, male and female literacy through educational institutions and new vocational skills. These were instrumental in changing the socio-economic life of the Khasis.

Along with the British came the "*dkhar*" (plainsmen) — as labourers, clerks, interpreters and government functionaries. They also brought with them new languages, religion and life-styles. The impact of this crisscrossing of different cultures, religions and languages on the tiny, isolated Khasi community has been tremendous. A complete sea-change came about in almost all areas of life, political, economic and socio-cultural within a space of fifty years or so, the once isolated rural communities have been hurled into the world of bigger, more modern, and technologically advanced societies and into the civilizations that are centuries old.

The Khasi society is still reeling under the impact, trying to stand as single identifiable group in a sea of diverse races and culture without being assimilated by the more dominant group. As a society in transition, it is still suffering from the traumas and tensions as it strives to retain its identity, and at the same time it moves on to become a modern literate society within the bigger, yet somewhat alien concept of a 'nation'. Keeping pace with the technological and electronic age has sapped the society of its strength. To add to the pressure is the tendency to cling on to its ancient and customary practices, some of which may be no longer relevant or feasible.

The preservation of a distinct identity in the midst of an enormous tide of influx, is a near impossible task. Such a great strain is bound to leave inevitable effects on the society. Transitional societies are dynamic, i.e., in a state of flux. Being unstable, they are perhaps more susceptible to influences which may come from outside, as a result of societal contacts, or from within, as a reaction to these changes. The amount of permeability of societies to changes will probably depend on (i) the strength of social cohesion and solidarity of that particular society, (ii) the strength of pressures for changes from outside, (iii) the strength of pressures for changes from inside. As mentioned earlier, pressures for changes from outside on the Khasi society have been tremendous. These have in turn weakened internal social mechanisms that have survived for centuries. The resultant effects are the lessening of social solidarity and the increasing of pressures for changes from within. To substantiate this point we will examine the Khasi family structures, and their resultant changes.

Khasi Concept of Family and Family Structures

Like most small tribal groups, the Khasis have survived as a community because of a complex network of family structures and relationships which bind the families, the clans (*Kur*), and the tribe together into a socially cohesive whole. Khasi being a matrilineal society gives primary importance to relationships with the matrilineal kin. Lineage and descent are traced through the female. Inheritance is confined to the matri-kin. The family structures consist mainly of the matri-kin members. They form a residential unit, as well as a socio-economic group. The Khasi families, have been bonded together by the household religion. In stressing the importance of the matri-kin, we are not to undermine the importance and role of relatives from the father's side, especially that of the father himself as the progenitor (*ukpaki khun*, or the father of children), paternal grandmother (*mei-kha* or 'mother-birth'), paternal grandmother (*parad*), paternal uncles (*pasan, pekhynnah*) and paternal aunts (*kha*). These relationships through marriages are important for social cohesion and solidarity. These ties closely knit one individual to another, and one *kur* to another *kur*.

To understand the Khasi concepts of 'family', we need to postulate different levels of family structures. They are given here.

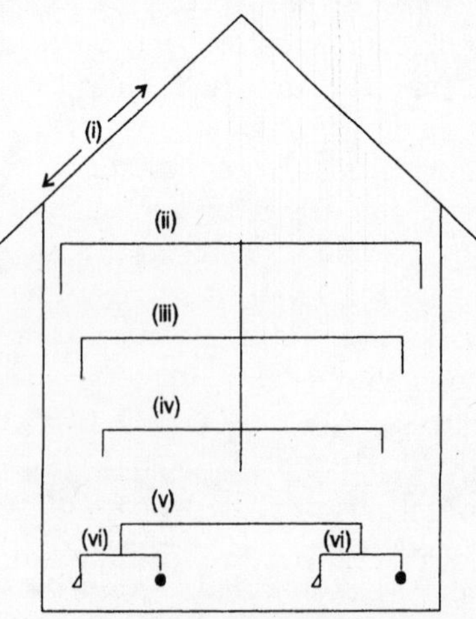

A diagram of family levels

i) *Hynniewtrei-Hynniewskum* (Khasis)
ii) *Ka Kur* (clan) and *Iawbei Tynrai* (root ancestress)
iii) *Ka Jait* (sub-clan), *Iawbei Tymmen* (old ancestress) and common surname.
iv) *Ka Kpoh* (lineage) and *Iawbei khynraw* (young ancestress).
v) *Ka Iing* (family), common *Meirad Tymmen* (great grand mother) and *Meiieit* (grand mother)
vi) *Ka Iing-Tnat*,[2] common *Mei/Kmie* (mother).

The smallest unit (level vi) termed here as *Iing-tnat* (literally branch-family) is the elementary family or household. Though the concept of an elementary or nuclear family has always existed, it is unclear why there is no separate word used for this family unit. The word *Iing* is conterminous for the family structures at level (v) and (vi). It can be hypothesized that in traditional Khasi society in the past, nuclear families were almost non-entities as independent units. Each household was linked to a bigger unit i.e., a corporate group of married sisters and their families, whose epicentre was the *Iing-kur* also called *Iing-Seng* (foundation-house) or *Iing Khadduh* (house of the youngest daughter). When the daughters other than the youngest and the sons marry, they were usually exhorted to establish their own families (*ban seng ia la ka Iing*) with parental or family help if possible such as the allotment of a plot of land, or the gift of some money. In such cases residence became neo-local. In the case of the youngest daughter, her husband came to reside her in the natal home.

The smallest family unit or household consists of the mother, father and their offsprings. It is a nuclear family structure in terms of co-residence, sharing common resources and fulfilling family roles, e.g., the father as provider (*u kpa uba lah uba ia*) and the mother as house-holder and keeper of the home (*kmie ka Iing*). In the case of the youngest daughter (*ka khadduh*), the family unit also includes her parents, widowed or divorced or single brothers and sisters, or any member of the *Iing* who has fallen into bad times. In a way, the *Iing* at the natal house is a joint family.

All married sisters and cousin sisters on the mother's side and their families, along with the *Iing-seng* or *Iing-khadduh*, constitute *Ka Iing*. They are descendants of a great grandmother, and are closely related. All the sisters of the mother are also *Mei* (mother). They are addressed depending on their birth order, *Meisan* (older mother), *Meideng* (middle mother), *Meinah* (young mother), and *Meiduh* (last mother). Their spouses are *Pa* (father), *Pasan, Padeng, Panah, Paduh* and so on. First cousins from the mother's side are "*shi-para arkmie*" (brothers and sisters from two mothers). Maternal grand parents are *Mei-ieit* (literally, love-mother) and *Pa-ieit* (love-father). These kinship terms stress the fact of an 'extended' family consisting of many mothers, fathers, brothers and sisters. The mother's brothers (*ki kni*), have great authority in the extended Iing. They are addressed appropriately as *Maheh* or *Ma Rangbah* i.e. big or oldest uncle, *Madeng* (Middle uncle), *Makhynnah* (young uncle) and *Maduh* or last uncle. They act as advisers, counsellors, mediators, and helpers in times of need (*u kni ha ka iap ha ka im*, i.e., the maternal uncle in times of life and death). This closely-related *matrikin* unit forms a domestic, socio-economic and religious intra-group community. The *Iing* can be understood as an extended family without members being co-residential.

Certain binding forces and familial symbols served to knit the members of the *Iing* together. They are: (1) A common (great) grandmother. (2) The number of households within a specific matrilineal descent group, and all members herein. (3) Common ancestor cult. (4) Common household deities and household religion. (5) Common 'priest' in the oldest maternal uncle (*kni rangbah*). (6) Common *Iing Seng* or *Iing Niam* (literally, 'House-religion') as a sanctuary. (7) Common ancestral property (if any).

All members of a descent group trace their descent to a great-grandmother who, if still alive, resides in the natal house or *Ing-Seng*. The parental/ancestral house is the centre of all family affairs, including religious rites and rituals. This *Iing* also represents a sanctuary, a place of family worships and rituals, as well as a place of refuge. It is a place where the larger extended family gathers in times of joy and in times of sorrow, in lighter moments for the warmth of kith and kin, and in weightier moments for crucial family decisions, calamities, death and sickness.

The Functions of the *Iing*

1. The *Iing* functions as a social community which gathers members together for all family events, religious or otherwise. Social relations within the descent group of the *Iing* are also maintained by regular visits among family members. When the nuclear families constituting the *Iing* are within reasonable distances, it is quite common for families of married daughters and sons to 'drop in' for a plate of rice or a cup of tea, either at the *Iing Khadduh* or in each other's families. Next to the nuclear family, the *Iing* functions as a basic social group where children are socialized.
2. Older members of the *Iing* have the important duty of imparting moral and social instructions (*ka snęng ke kraw, ka kdew ka pyni*) to the young. *Ki Jinganeng Tymmen* (old people's instruction) include, codes of conduct, social etiquette and manners and customary practices.
3. The *Iing* also functions as a welfare organisation. The aged, the destitute, the handicaped, the orphaned and the widowed are all taken care of by those who are fit and productive. The natal house or *Iing kur* is a place of refuge, and one of the duties of the *Khadduh* is to look after such members and to distribute pooled resources for their welfare. It is unthinkable for any *Iing* to leave any of its members uncared for, hence beggars as such are unknown among the Khasis.
4. Khasi religion being basically a house-hold religion, the *Iing* functions as a religious unit. Members gather together in the *Iing-Niam* on occasions like births, naming ceremonies, engagements, wedding, deaths, bone interment, and other rituals like *ka knia Ai bam and ka phen ka kyrpad* as propitiation to household deities. The seniormost uncle (*kni rangbah*) usually acts as the family priest, while the duty of the *khadduh* is to prepare the necessary items for the rites and rituals. She epitomises the family religion, and is referred to as the one who "keeps the religion" (*kaba bet ia ka niam*). However, the *khadduh* is not a "priestess" as wrongly stated

by many writers, since she does not actually perform any ceremony.

5. The *Iing* functions as an economic unit in the distribution and sharing of land, resources and family property. The *Iing* may own some land or common property which may be used or divided among all constituent nuclear families. It is common for an *Iing* having some land, to allot plots to married daughters so that they can set up their own families. The sons are also given property for their use. The *khadduh* is the custodian of ancestral property for common use; she is not an "heiress" as wrongly reported in the literature. The actual management of ancestral or common property is in the hands of maternal uncles who are the executive authority in the matri-kin group. If the *Iing* does not have enough or any property, the *khadduh* may be the one who is in need of help from more prosperous sisters. In such cases, the position of the *khadduh* is far from enviable, since she has to bear the *Iing's* burdens.
6. The *Iing* functions as a family council or '*durbar*' where maternal uncles (*kni*), grand parents, parents (*ki kmie ki kpa*) and older members of the family deliberate about marriages, deaths, family rituals, property and other family affairs. In the past the maternal uncles were vested with higher authority and power than the other members. They are advisers, managers, and executives of family affairs. However, women members too have power in decision making.
7. Finally the *Iing* functions as a political unit, since senior male members especially the *kni*, usually represent the *Iing* in the clan council (*Durbar kur*).

The management and execution of all the above social, religious, economic and political functions, is made possible by the usual residential patterns in the past. The constituent households or nuclear families were usually in the same village, or even in the same hillock or compound. At the most, they were scattered only within the nearby villages. This close physical proximity of families not only gave a sense of oneness, but made it possible for the *Iing* to function as a larger family unit. The members too were emotionally attached to one another.

Ka kpoh specifies a family consisting of all descendants of *Ka Iawbei khynraw* (young ancestress). They are of the same lineage; blood relationship is real and the degree of kinship is traceable, though not as close[14] as among members of the *Iing*. It is extremely difficult to arrive at any definite conclusion regarding the generational depth of its members. The Khasis do not keep written records of geneaological lines, but trace their descent to whatever generation that they are likely to remember, usually upto five-six generations. Kinship terms across generation can perhaps throw some light on this. There is no kinship term to indicate persons beyond five generations. Unlike the *Iing*, the *Kpoh* is not a functional unit, though close ties are maintained whenever possible, such as sickness, marriages, deaths and bone burial.

Nakane has defined the *kpoh* as a group of matrilineal *kin* usually confined to one domestic family or group of households, linked by direct extension of the main household. She also perceives the *kpoh* as a religious and ritual unit which shares a household religion as well as a common grandmother or great grandmother.[3] Gurdon states that the Khasis when reckoning descent, count from the mother only; they speak of a family of brothers and sisters, who are the great grand children of one great grandmother as *shi kpoh*, which literally translated, is one womb, i.e., the issue of one womb.[4] However, both descriptions seem to refer to the Khasi *Iing* rather than the *kpoh*. Pakyntein observes that the *Iing* extends to five generations and the *kpoh* to ten generations.[5] Hence a common (great) grandmother upto four generations only, is not the ancestress of a *kpoh*, but of an *Iing*. Nongbri categorically states that the *kpoh* is not a functional unit but the Iing is.[6] However, Nongbri's observation that the *kpoh* comprises members born of a common great-grandmother may be reexamined.

Ka jait (sub-clan) is distinguished from *ka kur* (clan) in that, all members of *ka jait* share a common surname or jait which traces back to the *Iawbei Tymmen* (old ancestress). The surname may have been derived from her first name, or something connected with her, or a place to which she migrated.

Though descendants claim a common origin in *ka Iawbei Tymmen*, the degree of kinship is not traceable, and blood relationship is mostly fictive. Members of *ka jait* may have been scattered throughout the Khasi Hills. Sometimes degree of kinship is reckoned to be close if members of a *jait* come from the same village. Interestingly, whenever Khasis meet as strangers, they will invariably enquire about the jait or surname of each other. If they happen to be in the same jait, further questioning will reveal if they are close kin.

Ka kur (clan) constitutes the macro-family structure binding the different *jait, kpoh* and *Iing* into a social family. There are three types of *kur* formation:

(a) Members trace descent to a first ancestress or founding mother, *Ka Iawbei Tynrai* (literally, "root" ancestress).
(b) Members may not share a common *Iawbei Tynrai*, but by the process of kur-binding (*iateh kur*) in the olden days, some *jait* (sub-clans) are bound by covenants to be in one *kur*, though they have different *jait* and different origin.
(c) Woman brought from outside e.g. from the plains, became integrated into Khasi society by establishing new clans, usually called by names derived by their first names and suffixed with the word Dkhar (plainsman/woman), with the 'D' deleted, e.g. Dkhar & Rani = Kharrani.

Blood relationship at the *kur* level is fictive; hence kinship is not traceable. However, clan exogamy is strictly observed by all members, whatever be their *jait* or degree of kinship. *Ka bynsieh ka byrnaang* (pollution) and *ka sangiap ka sangim* (incest of the worst kind) are terms referring to incestuous relationship if members of the same *kur* marry. This emphasises the concept of the *kur* as a larger family. The idea of incest could have dated back to a far past when the *kur* was small, and members were kinsmen with real blood ties. However, all the core symbols of clan unity and the *kur* as a macro family structure remain. They are the clan cromlech (*Mawbah, Pepbah, Mawiam*), a supposedly common *Iawbei Tynrai*, a common *Thawlang* (the primodial progenitor, husband of *ka Iawbei*), a common *Suidria* (the primodial maternal uncle) who established the religion of the clan, a common

Lei lang kur Leilangkha (god/goddess of the *kur* and *kha* = i.e. maternal and paternal sides), a common land (*Ri-kur*), a clan council (*Durbar kur*), and clan elders (*Rangbah kur*) and so on. Symbolic kinship terms for clansmen/women such as *Ma, Meisan, Meihah* and *Meirad* are sometimes used even when kinship is fictive. Another aspect of the *kur* in Khasi matriliny is its embodiment in Khasi religion, as *ka niam tip kur tipkha* (a religion that knows its maternal and paternal kin). In other words, the concept of *kur* is so ingrained in the Khasi mind, that it has been elevated to the level of the sacred, a part and parcel of Khasi religious philosophy. "The Khasi religion, to some extent, is a formalization and encoding, in religions terms, of the kinship code, and of the family and social structures. . . ."[7]

At the highest level, there is the Khasi concept of a "universal" family of *ki khun Khasi khara* (children of the Khasi). The folktale of *ka Jingkieng Ksiar* (The Golden Bridge) which linked the heaven and the earth, when distinctions between gods and men were blurred, recalls the days of *ki aiom ksiar* (golden seasons/times). The Khasi 'universal' family of *ki Hynniewtrap Hynniewskum* (seven huts and seven nests) comprises all Khasis who trace their origin to the heavenly abodes. At this level divine origin is the source of life, and not an ancestral womb. However, the concept of "family" oneness is borne out by expressions like *para khasi khara* (fellow Khasis) *paradoh para anam* (of the same flesh and blood) or *ki khun ki ksiew u Hynniewtrep* (children and grandchildren of the seven huts). This macro "family" functions at the societal level, where the "family" is the whole society or community of fellow Khasis and *Pnars.* This is the ultimate binding force of the whole tribe.

The hierarchical structures of "family" strengthen the sense of unity and oneness, tracing common descent at different levels. Khasi family[5] structures have provided the in-built mechanisms for social cohesion, solidarity, peaceful co-existence, economic welfare and prosperity, and ultimately, for survival. The importance of the concept of family and the kinship code can be gauged from the fact that it has become a creed in the Khasi religion as *ka niam tipkur tipkha.*

Changes in the Khasi Family Structures and Functions

Nakane and Gough are some of the writers who have pointed out the structural weakness in matriliny. The term "matrilineal puzzle" refers to the inherent conflicts in matriliny. Nakane states that "the complexity of the matrilineal system is a decided handicap when it comes to resisting radical economic changes. This may be one of the reasons for the rapid disintegration or instability of social organisation of matrilineal peoples in the world."[8] Gough's observation is in the same strain "matrilineal groups seem to be badly hit as soon as their members enter the market system. Although they may not disintegrate altogether for many decades, they are likely to break down to their minimal segments . . . . Patrilineal descent groups seem better able to weather the early changes."[9] Similarly, Poewe believes that "The contradiction between the increasingly social nature of the forces of production and the still private character of appropriation creates the material conditions for the disappearance of the system."[10] Khasi society too is in the process of transition from the agrarian subsistence economy to a market economy. As such it is bound to be susceptible to social changes. Besides economic reasons, many scholars have noted that in matrilineal societies there are basic structural contradictions such as:

1. The tension between the individual (nuclear) family and the matrilineal descent groups (e.g. *Iing, kpoh* in the Khasi context).
2. The conflict between a man's loyalties to his wife and children and his loyalties to his own matrikin. This conflict of natal and conjugal loyalties also applies to the woman (especially the *khadduh*).
3. The conflict between marriage and sibling cohesion.
4. The conflict between ownership and authority e.g., land and property are in the names of female members, but authority is with the males. Again the *khadduh* symbolically "keeps" the religion (*ka bat ia ka niam*), but *kni Rangbah* performs the rites.
5. The conflict between matrilocal residence and a man's lack of complete authority over his own conjugal family.

6. The conflict between productive individualism and communal distribution.
7. The conflict between two sets of heirs (a man's children, and his neices/nephews).

Poewe states, "Even at the best of times, matriliny embraces contrary sets of values."[11] Matriliny as a system is ridden with structural contradictions. Khasi matriliny too has been put under tremendous strain by rapid change in all spheres of life as outlined earlier. This has the inevitable effect on the family structures, especially the extended family or *Iing*, which is an integral part of the Khasi matrilineal system. The *Iing* as a corporate descent group is increasingly non-functional. The *Iing* as a family has to a large extent disintegrated or at the point of disintegration.

Many Khasis have migrated to cities in search of education, jobs or a better way of life. In many villages, those who are left behind are only the old, the uneducated and the handicapped. The result of urbanisation and migration is that members of the *Iing* are scattered everywhere, not only to the four corners of the state, but outside too. Hence, the functions of the *Iing* as a family unit are no longer feasible nor practicable. The controlling authority vested on the maternal uncles (*kni*) has become ineffective. In many cases, the neices and nephews do not even see their uncles, except at some important family gatherings.

Changes in patterns of residence from matrilocal to neolocal have created a new phenomemon of independent households or elementary family units, where the father and mother, bear the sole responsibilities for their offsprings.

Education and new occupations, especially 'white' and 'blue' collar jobs, have created a new elites and new socio-economic classess in what was an egalitarian society. This has an effect on the *Iing* as divisions based on economic and social standing have put members of the *Iing* apart.

The change from subsistence economy to market economy has led to privatisation of resources. Individualism and privatisation have made people more self-centred, hence the function of the *Iing* as welfare unit, with common appropriation of resources, has become nominal. The influence of modern-day materialism and consumerism has considerably weakened the give-and-take relationship of members within the *Iing*. Accumulation of wealth, rather than distribution to needy kith and kin, is now the order of the day. Conflicts between the controlling *kni*, the *khadduh* as custodian, (but increasingly like an " inheritor"), other siblings and members of the matrikin, are vouched by numerous court cases and litigations. Conflicts may also arise between a *Iing Khadduh* and a *Iing khun* (i.e., the natal and conjugal families) in appropriating a man's earning or possessions. As Schneider has rightly observed, "An increase in conjugal family solidarity and loyalty is likely to be at the expense of the economic solidarity of matrilineal ties."[12]

New religions or the lack of any religion in non-believers, have rendered, the practices of household religions ineffective which have been the binding force of the *Iing*, the *kpoh* as well as the *kur*. The *Iing-Seng* or *Iing-Khadduh* as a family sanctuary (*Iing-Niam*) binding the *Iing, kpoh* and *kur* together, is either nominal or non-existent. This is especially true for the urbanised Khasis, for whom the ancestral home is far away in remote villages. Secondly, very few Khasis (even those who practise *Ka Niam Khasi*) observe all rituals, especially those related to sacrifices. The practice of bone internments in the *Mawshyieng*, or *Mawbah* is observed by fewer still, partly because of the huge expenses incurred and partly due to various other reasons. The expression *Ngi La sah khynnah* (we are left as children) sums up the inabilty to continue the old practices.

The influx of partilineal societies, and inter-religious marriage have greatly weakened the Khasi concept of family, especially the matrilineal descent groups of the *Iing* and the *kpoh*. Cross-cultural influence of partilineal societies tend to orient the present generation to the conjugal, nuclear family rather than to the *Iing*. Processes of modernization in a transitional society and resultant changes in all spheres of life bring with them the added strain on matrilineal descent groups.

The changes and disintegration of matriliny have inevitable repurcussion which results in the following:

The nuclear or elementary family has emerged as a more important family unit in terms of residence, economic co-operation, socialisation, responsibility, welfare and moral well-being. In fact, *Iing* as usually applied in the modern days, especially in urban areas, is the elementary family termed *Iing-tnat* in this paper. There is also a trend for strengthening the conjugal family's solidarity.

There is decline in avuncular authority though the emergence of paternal authority is still an unusual concept among the Khasis, since women take on important authoritative roles and are usually involved in all decision making processes. The position, status and locus of authority of Khasi men are shifting from the natal to the conjugal home, and they are becoming more *kpa* than *kni*. Except in the case of a *khadduh* of a family owning a house, residence in most cases tends to be neolocal. This is especially true in urban areas. There is a decisive weekening of ties among members of a descent group. The term '*ki kur ja kur doh*' (clansmen only during special occasions) distances relatives from the same *kur*. The growth in numbers as well as other factors have made clansmen almost like strangers. Socialization is no longer restricted to cognates (*kur*) but includes agnates (*kha*). There are trends for changes in kinship terms especially in urban, educated settings, e.g. *Mai* (mother) refers to the grandmother, *Mi* (a contraction of Mummy') refers to a mother.

Conclusion

The *Iing* as a family structure has disintegrated or is in the process of disintegration. It follows that the functions of the *Iing* are no longer operable. It also logically follows that the next higher structure, i.e., the *kpoh*, has also disintegrated to a large extent. Khasi matriliny in this sense is similar to the fourteen disintegrating matrilineal societies examined by Gough, such as the Tongs, Ndembu, Bemba, Ashanti, Hopi, Minangkabau and so on.[13] As Gough has rightly pointed, variations may exist in the steps, in the process, and in the degree of change; however, the end results are the same.

It has been stated at the beginning that the amount of a society's permeability and its susceptibility to change depends on several factors. As a matriliny society, Khasi matriliny has weak structural foundations which became shaky when confronted by rapid socio-economic changes. As a traditional society moving towards modernisation, the Khasi society is being reshaped by those changes. The fluid and fluctuating nature of such a society has in turn weakened the foundations of the Khasi family structures at all levels, espcially the *Iing* and the *kpoh*. The disintegration of the *Iing*, consequently of the *kpoh* and *kur* as strong forces of social cohesion, negates the sense of solidarity and oneness, and the tie of social cohesion. Pressures for changes from inside are in the process. For example, some organisations and individuals are questioning the validity of the matrilineal system in the present time. Only time will tell whether the whole system of matriliny will give way to inevitable changes.

NOTES AND REFERENCES

1. Henceforth, the term 'Khasi' will be used as inclusive of the *Khynrien, Pnar, Bhoi* and War sub-groups. Slight dialectal and cultural variations may exist, but the basic matrilineal features are the same.
2. For want of a term, the word has been coined, in order to distinguish the elementary or nuclear family from the smaller extended family which is at the next higher level. In common usage both the elementary and the extended family are called *Iing* family, home or house. In the literature the word 'household' has been used to refer to this small family unit which includes the affines as well.
3. Nakane, Chie, *Garo and Khasi, A comparative study in Matrilineal Systems,* Mouton & Co., Paris. 1967.
4. Gurdon, P.R.T., The *Khasis,* Cosmos Publication, New Delhi.1975 (First Published in 1907).
5. Pakyntein, V., "The Khasi Clan: Changing Religion and its Effect" in Bhandari J.S., (ed.) *Kinship and Family in North-East India.* Cosmos Publication, New Delhi, 1996.
6. Nongbri, T., "Problems of Matriliny: A short Review of the Khasi kinship structure", in Bhandari, J.S. (ed.), Vol. II, Cosmos Publication, New Delhi, 1996.
7. War, J., "Status of Women in Traditional Khasi Culture", in Sen, S. (ed.). *Women in Meghalaya,* Daya Publishing House, Delhi, 1992, p. 20.
8. Nakane, Chie, op. cit. p. 43.
9. Gough, K., "Modern Disintegration of Matrilineal Disintegration of Matrilineal Descent groups", in *Matrilineal; Kinship,* D.M. Schneider and K. Gough (ed.), University of California Press, Berkeley, 1961. p. 649.
10. Poewe, L.O., *Matrilineal Ideology, Male-Female Dynamics in Luapala, Zambia,* Academic Press, London, 1981. p. 120.
11. Ibid p. 119.
12. Schneider D.M. (ed.). Ibid. p. 16.
13. Gough, K., loc. cit.

4

The Khasi Matriliny: Its Past and Its Future

Sohblei Sngi Lyngdoh

History as a whole is by nature dynamic. Because of this inherent dynamism, history relentlessly moves on towards that God-intended fulfilment of the Universe and of the human race. We have called it "inherent", because it springs up from within history itself; it is its 'elan vital', a living force permanently implanted by the Creator Himself for a definite purpose that can never fail to be eventually and fully realized. Thus, once history has begun, it keeps on gathering its inevitable momentum and infallibly reaches its goal. Hence the human race, taken as a unit, cannot but dynamically move on towards its intended fulfilment. And this happens so because the human race as such timely and readily fits itself within the overall circumstances and vicissitudes of history. But the human race, though taken as a whole is a unit, nevertheless is made up of different nations, races and tribes. Now as a matter of fact, not all the different nations, races and tribes have been capable of fitting in themselves adequately in the various events and situations of history. Such being the case, history's dynamism does not operate in the same way in every nation, race and tribe. So, in accordance with the response given by these various human groups, history's dynamism manifests itself in its best in some, in others it does seem slow and sluggish, while still in others it may even seem inoperative. Hence, some nations, races and tribes, such as the Nagas and

Mizos, are thriving and flourishing, others, such as the Kotas, are languishing, while still others are fast disappearing, such as the Todas in Southern India.

The Khasis' need of the hour is to have a sincere look at themselves, at their traditions, laws and customs. Evidently, this is a vast subject. Since time and space do not permit us, we shall limit ourselves to the Khasis' family system. We personally are convinced that the Khasis' imperative need of the hour is to bring in line their traditions, laws and customs that directly concern their family with the present historical transformation.

Original Matrilineal System: The Importance of the Uncle

Like many races and tribes, such as the Nayars in Kerala and the Achiks in Meghalaya, the Khasis came to have matrilineal family system. When the Khasis adopted it, is difficult to say. Basing themselves on the not-yet-convincingly-proven opinion that the Khasis came from South East Asia or Cambodia, where there is no sign at all of the existence of this matrilineal family system, some scholars believe that the Khasis adopted their matrilineal family on their way in the hoary past to these hills. They believe that the Khasis did this in order to tide over some unexpected vicissitudes of history that threatened their very existence and survival. Whatever this might be, one thing is sure, the esteem and the love for this matrilineal system have sunk deep into their very marrow so much so that the Khasis in general have come to be convinced that this matrilineal system is their unique characteristic that distinguishes them from the rest of the human race. This belief is, of course, not true to facts because there are other races and tribes which did have and still have matrilineal system. According to some observers, the Khasi system seems to have fallen into a very precarious situation as it has lost a good part of its strong foundation. This is precisely the topic we would like to deal with in this short paper. In order that we may understand fully the transitional and precarious situation of the Khasis' matrilineal system, we shall now try to give a short description of its original form. We are still lucky and in time because the Khasi matrilineal system's original form still exists in many places in the Pnar Hills, particularly in Khliehriat area. This writer himself has met and spoken to some men in Lum Shyrmit, in Shamsham and in Narwan, who still follow the system in its original form.

In its original form, the constitutive elements of Khasis' matrilineal system are the following: (i) The Uncle as the centre of authority and economy, and (ii) the Uncle's sister with her children from a father from another clan, who has nothing to do with this family except procreation. In this system, the Uncle is the pivot around which the whole family revolves. First of all, the Uncle is the centre of authority over the whole clan or over one particular branch of the family. The Uncle's authority is supreme and undisputed. His sisters and her children are completely under his authority. They cannot possibly do anything without the uncle's knowledge and consent. Nay, in certain cases the uncle seems to have power over the life and death of his sisters, nephews and nieces. It is said that in ancient times, the uncle could beat even unto death his nephews or nieces who committed the grave sin of incest by marrying within the clan. This authority was given to him in order to safeguard the purity of the clan. The Khasis are very strict on this point. From the procreative point of view, no male element of the clan should in any way return to the clan. The purity of the clan is preserved when women marry men from outside their clan. Lastly, the uncle's authority is life-long, even in extreme old age. The Khasi uncle used to be a real disciplinarian. His word was law for his nephews and nieces in the past. Hence, the Khasis used to say, "The uncle has said so, or has decided so." To correct a disobedient child, the mother used to say, "I will inform the uncle." This phrase was enough in the past to correct any erring member of the family. Literally, the whip was ever ready in the hands of the Khasi uncles in the past. Lastly, the uncle is the administrator of all the goods movable and immovable, of the family or even of the whole clan. Of all the members of the family, the uncle is the chief earner and worker. The Khasi uncle administers principally the products of his toil and moil, of his sweat and perspiration. There is care and seriousness in this type of administration. With the uncle as the centre of economy, all the members of the family had to work and sweat. Nephews and nieces, above 15 years of age, had to be up and doing because of the ever-pricking goad: the uncle.

Now in contrast with the uncle, the father is an outsider, who has no authority, no control and no say whatsoever in the lives of his wife and children. He is only the respected, esteemed and appreciated procreator. As a matter of fact, the father is completely absent from his wife and children during the day. Only at night he is with his wife and not necessarily with his children. This situation of the father may make some people think that the Khasi male is nowhere in society. This is not true. It is true that the father is an outsider in his wife's house, but as an uncle in his sister's house he is really someone who has a recognized dignity and importance.

Now from religious point of view, the uncle is the priest, the teacher and the intercessor between God and his sister with her children. That is, the religion is in his hands too. He has to perform the yearly sacrifice for the whole family and also for the whole clan. When his nephews and nieces get sick, he has to divine the cause by cutting the cock or breaking the egg. If the cause is some grave sin committed by the members of the family *Daw iing* in Khasi, then the culprit has to confess either privately or even publicly to the uncle, who then would intercede with God for him in order to be pardoned. Here we see that the uncle is the confessor for his sister and his nephews and nieces. Lastly, the daily morning and evening prayers have to be conducted by the uncle. It is during these prayers that the uncle teaches, advises and exhorts his nephews and nieces to earn righteousness in their life, to cultivate virtues and lead a life worthy of their clan. The uncle's sister, as a mother, is the symbol of a Khasi family. Every mother, according to the Khasis' belief, re-enacts the life and role of the first Ancestress of the clan, lovingly called the "Divine Mother *Ka Blei Iawbei*". Hence, for the uncle, who is her elder brother, she is clothed and invested with an aura that is truly divine. If the mother is so in the eyes of her brother, her children too get an equal share of unconditional acceptance, regard and effective love. Hence, the uncle is inseparably linked to his sister and his nephews and nieces. The uncle can never disown his sister and her children nor can his sister and her children disown the uncle. In the past, it was never never known that a Khasi family was broken and destroyed. Whatever the father might do as an outsider, the uncle remains with his sister and her children all the time except for those few hours of the night when he goes to sleep with his wife in her house.

Family Fission

We have said above that the uncle's sister and her children are the constitutive element of the Khasis' original matrilineal system. Now some may ask, "What do we mean by sister ? Is she the so called *Khadduh* (the last daughter). She may be or she may not be. Let us take just one example. In a family there may be many children, both boys and girls. Suppose there are six children in a family born alternately boys and girls: A, B, C, D, E, F. So A, C and E are boys and B,D, F are girls. Evidently A is the first born boy. Consequently, when he comes of age, he becomes automatically the chief uncle with his brothers C and E as subaltern uncles. Hence, the term "uncle", as used above, includes the chief uncle (*Kni Rangbah*) and his brothers as subaltern uncles. Now ordinarily, in the Khasis' original matrilineal system, the eldest girl gets married first. In this example, the eldest girl is B. The term "sister with her children" includes B, her children and her other sisters as well. Evidently, the phrase "The uncle and his sister with her children" is just a mode of speech. In reality, the term "uncle", as noted above, includes the eldest brother as the chief uncle and his other brothers as subaltern uncles. Likewise, the term "sister with her children" means the eldest married daughter, her children, and all her sisters and their children.

As when, in due time, A, C and E get married, they do not go to live and work in their wives' house. They live and work in their sisters' house. Brothers and sisters, therefore, live together, work together and eat together. We do not mean that there is no partitioning of the family. As a matter of fact, partitioning of the family is part of the Khasis' matrilineal system. An example will illustrate point. We have said that in due time B, the eldest sister, has to get married in order to increase and multiply the family and the clan. When her children grow up and come of age and are capable of earning their livelihood, the family's partition takes place (*Mih iing*). B, as the eldest sister, has to move out to another house. As this is an important event in the family, it is never done all of a sudden nor haphazardly. A, as the chief uncle along with his brothers would see to it that that B has a well-built new house, enough means to live on and enough land to cultivate. Hence, B and her children are well provided by the uncle from the so-called self-acquired property of the uncle and of B and her children, and not from the ancestral property be it movable or immovable. The ancestral property has to remain with the uncle, his brothers and sisters who are still living together. As regards land, there was no problem in the past, as it was common land (raid land) and people could easily have the land they needed. Thus, well provided in accordance with human dignity, B, as the eldest sister, moves on to another house to start a new branch of the family or clan.

Now some may ask, "Who is the uncle in the new home of B, the eldest sister?" Evidently, A, as the eldest brother, continues to be the uncle until his death. Though B has moved to a different house, A, as the chief uncle now, has still the duty to supervise, to care and provide for B and her children. Thus A is committed for life to look after his sister B, even if his brother C were to opt to live with B and her children.

Now this process of partitioning the family carries on and stops only at the last sister F, who is the last daughter (*Khadduh*). As the last sister, F continues to live in the ancestral home with A as the chief uncle and his other brothers as subaltern uncles. Moreover, all the ancestral property is *de jure* and *ipso facto* handed over to F, not as to an absolute mistress, but as a guardian under the administration of the chief uncle. The ancestral property is owned by the whole clan as such. Hence, it belongs to B and D, as much as to F. Only the guardianship is handed over to F, as the last sister or daughter and not the ownership, which belongs to the whole clan. The motive behind this practice is that any member of the clan has a right to fall back on the ancestral property, if by some stroke of misfortune they happen to be in dire need. In such cases, the last sister or the last daughter is duty bound to share generously the usufruct of the ancestral property, of which she is only the guardian. Who is to judge whether a certain member of the clan is in dire need? The chief uncle studies the situation and in all fairness gives his ruling, which is binding and final. Hence, should B as the eldest sister fall into indigence, A as the chief uncle intervenes in order to provide B with such means of livelihood as befits a human being and he does this by generously giving B the usufruct of the ancestral property, of which F, as the last daughter, is the guardian.

Because of this peculiar economic practice of the Khasis' matrilineal system there were no indigent persons among them in the past. The blind, the deaf, the incurably sick and the orphans of the clan could rely, in the past, on the usufruct of the ancestral property and hence they were never left abandoned and uncared for. The last sister or the last daughter, as the guardian of the ancestral property, had the strict obligation to welcome and look after the members of the clan that were in dire and real need. Consequently, in the past, there were no beggars among the Khasis. There were no abandoned and uncared for orphans. The clan, with the chief uncle at the head, would see to it that no member of their can should be left indigent and neglected. Truly, in the original matrilineal system, the Khasi family or clan was a welfare state in miniature, since the one and chief pre-occupation of the chief uncle was that every member of the family or clan should be well provided with everything needed for a decent human life in dignity and honour.

Changing Family

But sad to say, at a certain time, long before the British conquest, the Khasis' matrilineal system began to give way to a change for the worse. According to this writer this change took place in histroy because the Khasis seemed to have forgotten one important law and principle of their social life and organisation. Tradition has it that in the Third Divine Assembly or *Durbar* held at the foot of Sohpetbnen Hill, this law was solemnly promulgated, "Whenever you start a new village or town, see to it that there are enough groups of cognates and of agnates (*ki kur bad ki kha*)." Hence, never was it known that in the remote past there were villages or towns where there were ten families of cognates and two families of agnates. In every village and in every town or capital, there was more or less an equal number of cognate and agnate families. This law was very wise indeed, because it helped the original matrilineal system to function well.

The uncle goes to his wife's house only at night for the purpose of procreation. He would leave his sister's house after supper, more or less at 6.00 or 7.00 p.m. Then early at dawn, he would slip off from his matrimonial couch and dash straight to his sister's house to begin the day. For this reason, in ancient times, Khasi men would never marry outside their villages or towns. And precisely that the men might marry in their own villages or towns, the above mentioned law was promulgated that in every village or town there should be more or less an equal number of cognate (*kurs*) and agnate (*ki kha*) families, since the Khasis were from times immemorial exogamous, and hence they could not marry within their cognate families, but only in the agnate families. Upto this day, it is a sacrilege for the Khasi men to marry within their clan, a sacrilege considered unpardonable here on earth and in the next as well.

But by some stroke of misfortune and vicissitude of history, this wise law began to be forgotten and quite a long time before the British conquest of India, villages and towns came into existence, in which there were, say, one hundred cognate families (*kurs*) and only one aganate family (*kha*). Evidently, one agnate family could not possibly supply wives for men from one hundred cognate families. Consequently, those men had to look for wives in some far villages or towns. Because of the distance, it was not possible anymore for men to go to their wives' houses in the evening and then to return early in the morning to their sisters' houses.

Consequently, the Khasis' original matrilineal system began to disappear slowly. The uncle began to disappear from his sister's house and from his nephews and nieces. The father began to stay with his wife and her children, but only as a tolerated outsider, since he is not the member of the clan. This was the situation, in which the Khasis found themselves even before the Biritish conquest of India. Their original matrilineal system was fast dwindling. Authority and discipline began to wane in the Khasis' homes; confusion, want and even poverty started showing their ugly heads. Because of the neglect of that wise law that villages and towns should have more or less an equal number of cognate and agnate families, most fathers of family were strangers to one another as they had grown up in different villages or towns. It took a long time for them to understand and appreciate one another. This writer himself was a witness of this sad situation. There was a small meeting of some fathers of family in Mawlai Phudmuri, in which this writer was present. In the course of a lively and serious discussion regarding a social problem, one old father of family curtly remarked, "You have been here only two years. What do you know of this village ? So, please sit down and listen to us who have been here years and years." Evidently, in such a situation, there is bound to exist an unwarranted superiority complex in the elderly fathers of family and an unmerited sense of inferiority complex in the younger fathers of family in practically all the villages of the Khasis at this very moment. A new comer through marriage is considered as an ignorant novice in his wife's village. For at least ten years or so, he has to keep quiet in village affairs. This situation makes people lose interest in the social affairs of the village. Consequently, at the moment, the Khasi villages are anything but well governed.

Now this fast deteriorating situation became worse with the British conquest of India. The British rulers did not fully understand the original matrilineal system, because when they came, the Khasis' original matrilineal system had already undergone changes. They took the Khasis' matrilineal system in its somewhat deformed shape and made it more and more deformed by their wrong interpretation of the role of the youngest sister or daughter. This wrong interpretation of the role of the last daughter adversely and drastically affected the Khasis' economy. The British rulers took the last daughter as the owner of all the ancestral property, movable and immovable. They did not realize that she was only the guardian.

Thus, the British eliminated the uncle from his sister's house by abolishing *de facto* his role as the administrator of the property. With this elimination he lost also his position as the centre of authority, and of discipline.

Impact of Christianity

At this juncture, we may ask, "what about Christianity, education or modernisation? Have not these exercised some influence on the Khasis' matrilineal system?" First of all, Christianity came as a positive boon and an uplifting asset. It came as the fulfilment of the religious aspirations of the Khasis' ancestors. In the Third Divine Assembly, as mentioned above, God promised to send the All-powerful, the All-perfect, the Exalted, the All-knowing One as an Incarnate King, born of a virgin mother (*U Blah u Baiai, u Syntai u Bulot, u Kynrem u Lyndan, u simpah simsong bad u Syiem Longdoh Oongpun*). From that time the Khasi religion became a waiting religion (*Ka Niam kaba ap Jingong*). This Promised One would come not to destroy or abolish, but to strengthen, to fulfil and to perfect the Khasi Religion and through religion the Khasis' human life on earth. The above-mentioned titles are all divine titles. They do not fit in with any human person except Jesus Christ, Who is truly the All-powerful, the All-perfect, the Exalted and the All-knowing One, an Incarnate King born of a virgin mother. Hence, while the Khasis, as a race, have rejected Hinduism, Buddhism, and Islam because they do not conform with the above-mentioned Divine Promise, they readily accepted the Good News of Jesus Christ as soon as it was proclaimed to them because they saw that in Jesus the Promise made by God to their ancestors was fulfilled. As a matter of fact, the coming of Christianity has strengthened the Khasi religion, has preserved forever and ever its seven pillars or foundation stones, such as the "Naming rite (Baptism), the strengthening of personality (Confirmation), the reviving of personality (the Anointing of the sick), the Altar and Sacrifice (the Eucharist), Forgiveness of sins (Reconciliation), Marriage (Matrimony) and Consecraion of Priests (Ordination). With the definite preservation of these seven pillars, the Khasi religion lives and thrives more fully in Jesus Christ. In reality, any Khasi Christian can say the he/she is still in the Khasi religion as revived fully and perfected by Jesus Christ. This is the reason why the Khasis, as a race, have readily taken to Christianity.

But as far as the matrilineal system is concerned, Christianity has not brought any change. It has left it as it found it. None of the various denominations of Christianity has ever felt the need of interfering in the Khasis' matrilineal system. Church leaders seem to have studiously avoided getting involved in the problem of the Khasis' matrilineal system. But some may say, that Christianity has done much in reshaping the Khasis' matrilineal system, because on wedding days the role of the father is extolled and highly appreciated. It is true that during the celebration of marriages, the role of father is extolled and rightly appreciated, but this is done because of the readings from the Bible that have to be commented on such an occasion; but that Church leaders do not ever mention the matrilineal system on such occasions. Christianity as such has not interfered in the matter of the Khasis' matrilineal system.

Impact of Modernisation

Now we come to education, which the majority of the Khasis have seriously taken to. Education too has not done anything significant to reshape the Khasis' matrilineal system. As far as our knowledge goes, children are not taught anything about it in class. Here too there is almost an absolute silence about it. Some teachers, both men and women, seem afraid of even mentioning the subject. So far no question has been asked in the various public examinations. Hence, as far as education is concerned the matrilineal system is an unknown subject. Such being the case, no serious discussion has ever been made in the class-rooms about it. Even modernisation does not seem to have had any impact on the Khasis' matrilineal system, except in its economic aspect. All agree that the Khasis' economy has changed. The salary earning fathers of family, whose earning does not depend on the ancestral property of their wives, have improved their position and role. Their wives and children have begun to look up to them as once they used to look up to the uncles. These fathers of family have begun to exercise some authority on their wives and children; they have begun to get control of the discipline of the children, thanks to their economic status. But fathers of family of this calibre are comparatively few. Hence, very many fathers of family, both educated and uneducated, have not yet acquired that sense of commitment to their wives and children and the economy of the family. This is evident from the numerous complaints of mothers that their husbands do not bring any money but that they spend it in the road-side taverns with their friends. Thus, because the uncle is no more in his sister's house and because the father does not bother about the economic well-being of his children, the mother and her children are oftener than not half-fed, and half-clad.

The Khasis' original family set-up is no more, except in some cases in the Pnar Hills and in the War area, especially in Nonghken village, where the Catholic Church elder is still following the original matrilineal system. Speaking in general, the uncle is no more with his sister and her children; he has gone far away either in mind or in body as well. He does not feed and clothe his nephews and nieces, who, in consequence, do not have anymore that reverential awe and an unconditional obedience, that once they had for him. In general, there is indiscipline among the boys in the present Khasis' families; in many homes adolescents do not obey their mothers; they easily drop out from school, roaming in idleness and falling into bad company and very many fathers of family just sit down and watch the fun. They do not dare correct or beat them even when there is need, for fear lest mothers would say, "Go beat your own nephew and nieces; these are not your nephews and nieces." Thus unruly boys go scot-free. All these things happen because the Khasi family system at the moment is in a transition period. Some even say that it is dangling in mid-air. The situation seems really bleak and the once clear blue sky of the Khasi race is overcast but not without silver linings. As far as their matrilineal system is concerned, the Khasis are at the CROSS-ROAD of their history, but not without clear indications or pointers. These promising silver linings and assuring pointers are clearly seen in the Khasis' AWARENESS of this present anomalous situation of their matrilineal system.

And this awareness is not some sort of a hazy feeling, casually expressed in conversations on the road or in market-places, but according to this writer, it is quite definite and articulate and entrenched in seriously written books. They believe that it is imperative for them now to look hard and intelligently at their situation. They are convinced that their traditions and institutions, their laws and customs, must be critically and dispassionately examined, weighed and measured on the sure balance of history. There is nothing sacrosanct in people's traditions and institutions. Hence it is not only good but imperative as well, to change them from time to time if the onward movement of history demands it. And they conclude that it is in this context of timely change that the wisdom and dynamism of a nation, race or tribe, are clearly seen. And they are proud that this has actually taken place. This is a really good omen, a multi-coloured rainbow that infallibly promises a truly fair weather in the near future.

The Future of the Khasi Matriliny

The Khasis as a race sincerely and dispassionately ask these questions, "What shall we do then? Shall we change or shall we not change?" At the moment three answers have been given. Some say, "We must not change. We must keep our matrilineal system as it is our uniquely distinguishing mark." And they proudly expatiate on the beauty and grandeur of the matrilineal system. But as far as this writer's knowledge goes, none of this group has specified which type of their matrilineal system they want to preserve. This writer believes that they mean the matrilineal system in its original form in which the uncle stays in his sister's house. However, they are fully aware that the uncle is no more in his sister's house. Such being the case, their desire is just a fond but fruitless velleity.

Others, such as the members of Ka Syngkhong Rympei Thymmai (Association for new hearths), are of the opinion that the Khasis must change their matrilineal system into that of patrilineal set-up, in imitation of the Nairs of Kerala.

Evidently, this group does not think and does not speak of the original matrilineal system, as it does not exist anymore. They believe that what has ceased to exist, does not deserve any attention or discussion on it. Hence, what this group wants to change is the present "unhistorical" form of the Khasis' matrilineal system. At present there is no centre of real authority and economy in the Khasis' home. The father stays now in his wife's house with his children, but still as an outsider, though he is loved, esteemed and appreciated. He has no share in his wife's religion, if she happens to be in the Khasi Religion. In short, the father is not yet part and parcel of the family. The Khasis believe that the uncle, his sister and her children form one unit of flesh and blood as derived from the first ancestress. The father has no relation of flesh and blood with his wife and children. The children get from the father only his 'personality' (*Rngiew*) and his 'human dignity' (*ka rynieng ryniot*), but not his flesh and blood. The wife receives nothing from her husband, least of all his flesh and blood; hence, they can marry. Were the wife to get anything of the flesh and blood of the husband, their marriage would be an incest and a sacrilege.

To solve this difficulty, this second group considers the father and mother as one element and the children the other element. The father and mother constitute an inseparable unit by the marriage covenant as demanded by nature. Between the father-mother unit and that of the children there is a true relation in flesh and blood. The father gives not only his personality and dignity to his children, but his very flesh and blood through his seed in procreation. Nay, they argue that the flesh and blood relationship between the father and the children is more real and stronger than between the uncle and his nephews and nieces, who are begotten from another man. Here the second group finds its reason for transferring the role of authority and discipline to the father, who now lives, works and eats with his children. This group goes even a step further: they firmly believe that the relationship between the children and the father "through his seed" is so exceptionally important that they consider it right and just to trace even the descent from the father. Lastly, there is a third group of Khasis, who would like to trace the descent of the children from the father and the mother: the boys from the father and the girls from the mother. In order to facilitate this way of tracing the children's descent, this third group believes that the marriage covenant should contain, not only the surrendering of man and woman as persons to each other, but also the mutual transfer of the title of their respective clan. So, when Mr. Khrawnusip Kharkongor marries Miss. Sharimai Shabong, they must be called Mr. Khrawnusip Kharkongor-Shabong and Mrs. Sharimai Kharkongor-Shabong.

Once a mother remarked realistically to this writer, "I am in deep trouble. Ever since we got our first child, my husband gives us nothing, not a naya paisa. In the third month of my first pregnancy, my husband left me and never showed his face till the time when our child was three or four months. When he came back, I did not want to accept him again, but he promised never to repeat his bad behavior. I believed him. But as soon as I was pregnant again, he left me all of a sudden one morning. He spends all his money on drinks and was often found drunk in Iewduh (market place)." This is not a solitary story. Very many Khasi women have passed and are passing through this terrible trauma in their life. And all this happens so because of the breakdown of the original matrilineal system.

So, from what has been said above, it is clear that there is at present a lively, sincere and dispassionate discussion by the Khasis themselves on their matrilineal system. They are not afraid of carefully re-examining and re-evaluating all their traditions and institutions. There is no doubt that, should some of their traditions and institutions turn out to be irrelevant to the global movement of history, the Khasis as a race will not fail to show themselves intelligent and courageous enough to make the necessary reforms. This is a good and comforting sign that the Khasis as a race are not yet deprived of that much-needed dynamism.

5

Religion and Matriliny in Khasi Society: Some Observations

I.M. Syiem

It has always been maintained that Khasi Society is based on the following tenets — *Ka tip Blei ka tip briew* (God conscious, man conscious) and *ka tip kur ka tip kha*, (knowing maternal kin and paternal kin). The word *tip* here does not just mean 'knowing' or 'reckoning' in a superficial way. It involves an intricate network of kinship relationships and sentiments, obligations, convictions and beliefs that weave Khasi society together. Another established fact is that Khasi society is a matrilineal society, that is, lineage and descent is traced through the mother. The presence and authority of maternal uncle as a major decision-maker in the affairs of the clan (*kur*) excludes the notion that Khasi society is a matriarchy as is believed by some. Unlike patriarchy where lines of descent and authority are traced through the paternal males, in Khasi matriliny, descent follows the female line while control especially in traditional society, predominantly rests with the maternal males. In both cases, the males are the major decision-makers.

Male domination can be seen in various areas of Khasi social life particularly in matters of state and village administration. With few exceptions, political administration has been an exclusive male prerogative. Even today, men are loath to include women in village or local *durbars*. Women's representation in politics and political activities is still insignificant.

The absence of codification of traditional laws and the decrease in power of the maternal uncle in a fast changing society have created a hiatus and confusion of who really 'owns' or controls property. It is fairly clear-cut in family situations where the maternal uncle is still considered the major decision-maker. Even then, cases pending in the District Council bear out the fact that the youngest daughter (*ka khadduh*) can still assert claims of ownership of ancestral property. In today's materialistic society, the question of who inherits and who manages property is pertinent. Property especially in terms of land has not only an added economic value but has a psycho-cultural and political aspect as well. The pressures of modern living has far reaching consequences on the traditional authority structure of maternal males especially regarding decisions in property matters. The situation calls not only for redefinition of roles but a re-evaluation of the concept of property ownership which is ambiguously couched as 'custodianship' a term which can and has been interpreted in many ways. With the influence of other patriarchal cultures and inter-cultural marriages, this area of male and female economic rights as prescribed by tradition in a modern social context is fraught with tension and abuse.

Matriliny and Traditional Beliefs

There is another area where men's role and women's importance have not been fully explored, that is, religious role in the context of matriliny. Within the limitations of this paper, we only hope to highlight certain problems in the inter-relationship between matriliny and religion. Further research in this area will give more insight into the intricate networking of *ka tip kur*, *ka tip kha* and the world of convictions, beliefs, rituals and practices. The traditional religion of the Khasis is not an organized religion, though the Seng Khasi movement has given it a more formal and organized shape. No doubt it has a certain organized set of beliefs and practices which are universally recognized and accepted in Khasi society. There is certainly a large tradition, a large culture of legends and beliefs that have influenced the 'little traditions'. Religious activity and beliefs, however, by and large function at the local and family level. They are limited to meet the requirements of a small social and physical environment.

For our purpose here, we can consider religion as a system of beliefs and practices by which a group of people interpret and respond to what they feel sacred and usually supernatural as well.[1] (We are neither denying nor affirming the existence of the supernatural. We are only noting the fact that people in groups do in fact believe in the supernatural and consider certain things as sacred.) Within the scope of this definition we include not only the traditional beliefs and practices of the Khasis, but also other activities that deal with the supernatural. No village community is without its religious specialists, its 'diviners', also known in religious terminology as 'spiritist practitioners'. These mediators who deal with the supernatural are also found in the urban setting. In times of sickness, misfortune, when articles are lost or when there is a need to pray for good crop or success in jobs and business or even in elections, these diviners are consulted (most often with payment).

Interpreters and writers of Khasi society point out that the Khasi religion (*Ka Niam*) is the religion of the clan (*Kur*) and of the family (*Ka Kpoh ka ïng*). The family here is used in the wider sense of the matrilineal lineage (*Ka kpoh*—literally from the 'womb' of a particular mother going back to four or five generations). The fact that the oldest maternal uncle functions as the 'spiritual mediator' or priest (*U Lyngdoh*) of the family points out the fact of 'exclusive family worship'. To quote from O. Mawrie "*U long kñi ha ka ïng u long u lyngdoh u ban pyndep ia ki niam ki rukom baroh bad u leh ïa kita baroh ha ïng seng ïng khadduh.*"[2] (It is the maternal uncle who is the spiritual representative or the priest in the home who must fulfil all the religious requirements, rituals and customs and he does this in the *khadduh's* home which is also the ancestral home.) The *Mawbah* (family sepulchre for internment of bones) is another concrete fact that symbolizes the spiritual unity, apart from other things, of the clan (*kur*) at whatever level of its integration and unity.

The youngest daughter (*Ka khadduh*) has this function '*ka bat ia ka niam*', literally 'the keeper of the religion'. She has sometimes been interpreted as the priestess of the family.

She no doubt assists and prepares whatever is needed for performing religious activities. What is important to point out here is the deeper implication of the term '*Ka bat ïa ka niam*'.

We have already pointed out that Khasi society is based on the network of relationship between God and man (*Ka tip briew, ka tip blei*) and on the kinship relationship (*Ka tip kur, ka tip kha*). Religion is in fact inseparable from the kinship system, to be more specific, from the Khasi matrilineal system. In O. Mawrie's words "*U Khasi u seng bad u sain ïa ka niam ha la ka kur ka kur bad ha la ka jait ka jait. Ka kur pat ka pynshat ïa ka niam ha ka Blei, ka Iawbei, U Thawlang bad u Suidnia.*"[3] (In essence this means that the Khasis establish religion on the family and the clan. That religion revolves round the deity, the ancestral mother, the ancestral father and the ancestral maternal uncle.)

In prayer, the Khasi often calls upon '*ko Blei ko Iawbei* (God and Grandmother). Both are responsible for the well-being of that particular clan (*kur*). In fact the matrilineal *kur* was believed to have been established by God the Creator and Dispenser (*U Blei Nongbuh Nongthaw*). It is religion, '*ka Niam*' that then acts as a seal for the preservation of the matrilineal lineage (*ka kpoh*) and the clan (*kur*).

To the Khasis, God has no gender. They explain their invocation of the various names of God as his attributes. According to them God serves a particular need. He appears to be either a female or a male. So he is '*U Leilongspah*' (God of prosperity) or '*Ka Leilongkur ka Leilongjait*' (Deity who increases and protects the clan, more specifically the matrilineal lineage). '*U*' is masculine and '*ka*' is feminine.

Ka '*Iawbei*' is the ancestral mother who establishes a particular lineage or clan (*ka kur ka jait*). She has the 'sacred trust' of increasing and ensuring the preservation of her '*kur*' with the sanction and help of '*ka Leilongkur ka Leilongjait*'. Her daughters, '*ki Iawbei Khynraw*' are handed over this 'sacred trust' of clan for perpetuation and preservation. The youngest daughter and the ancestral home '*ka ïng seng ïng khadduh*' is the focus of this spiritual heritage and unity. Since religious activities related to the unity, preservation and well-being of *Kur* (clan) centre around the *Khadduh* and her home, which is also the ancestral home, she can be seen as symbolically keeping alive the family ritual and worship, that is religion or '*Ka niam*'. She is, in this sense, the 'keeper of religion'.

The ancestral maternal uncle '*U Suidnia*' is the one who formally establishes and seals the sacred pact of God and man in family worship and rituals including the ceremonial internment of bones in the '*Mawbah*'. The ancestral father, is the Co-Creator — '*U Thawlang*' along with '*Ka Iawbei*' (the ancestral mother). The father provides for the children and bears the daily responsibility of caring for them — '*U Kpa u ba lah ba ïai*'. The maternal uncle shares the burden specially in matters of life and death — '*u Knï u ba lah ba ka ïap ka im*'. Whatever their various functions are, the main consideration is perpetuation and preservation of the clan which is believed to have been established by God himself. Interestingly, legends and oral traditions have it that ancestral mothers '*Ki Iawbei*' of several *kurs* have a supernatural origin. This strengthens the belief that *Ka Leilongkur, ka Leilongjait* (clan deity) is actively involved in the function of procreation and preservation of the clan, in essence, in the survival of the Khasi society. What we have established so far is the interdependence of matriliny and religious belief in Khasi society. In other words we can say Khasi religious belief or '*Ka niam*' is vital for the survival of the '*Kur*' and the Khasi society as a whole.

Christianity and Change: Some Questions about Matriliny

Christianity came on the scene with its patriarchal values and cultural concepts. First generation converts completely cut themselves off from practising the traditional religion. Many were ostracized and rejected by their '*Kur*'. But there does not seem to be any conflict with retaining matriliny. It is only in recent times that matrilineal tradition has faced some problems. The first challenge has come from Christianity and its patriarchal values. The majority of Christians do not see a conflict here. However, there is a growing number of younger Christian members who are beginning to re-evaluate the roles of men and women in the context of Christian teachings. Adam, according to Christian belief, was created first. The ideal is, specially in the nuclear families, that the man is fully responsible for family in all areas. He is the 'spiritual head' who leads his family in worship. In traditional, non-Christian families the maternal uncle is the spiritual mediator. This is to mention only one area where Christianity has brought about a change in perception and attitude among the Khasis.

The second challenge has come from growing exposure and interaction with patriarchal cultures. Khasi society has had interaction with other neighbouring cultures in the past. Ever since Independence, the Khasi locality has been increasingly open to the larger society. Besides, many Khasis have gone out of their homes to other parts of India and outside India for education, and employment. Because of cross-cultural marriages and for various other reasons some Khasi children, specially in the urban areas are using their father's clan name or both their father's and mother's clan names. Interacting with patriarchal cultures, it is simpler to say 'I am the son of Mr. so and so' than to refer to the mother's name. This is particularly relevant if the father has a higher status in the society than the mother, and is more well known in the society.

The third and most vital challenge has come from the system itself. In a modern, materialistic society, property ownership especially in terms of land has become an important consideration. Oral tradition and even customary laws are no longer strong enough to prevent property disputes within families. The younger generations are increasingly questioning the right of the *Khadduh* to be the main trustee of family property. The control of the maternal uncle is decreasing. The *Khadduh* with all that she stands for has become a 'vulnerable institution'. There is a general agreement that while the matrilineal name be retained, property should be equally divided among sons and daughters, or at least the 'will' system should be enforced to prevent disputes within the family.

The Khasi matriliny faces challenges from its own members. In 1990, *Ka Synkhong Rympei Thymmai* an organization whose main objective is to motivate the Khasi society to change from matriliny to patriliny, was established. The organization was born out of a genuine social response and reaction to the stress and strain that matriliny is facing in the modern context. This group which includes a few women as well, believes the answer to the ills of Khasi society is to change from matriliny to patriliny. Their popular spokespersons quote the Bible as their reference for their Christian community. The Christians', especially the urban Christians', responses have varied from outrage and indifference to tolerance, acceptance and support.

While there is a trend towards patriliny by some sections of Khasi society, Khasi beliefs and practices still exercise control over the larger population even among Christians. We are referring to second and third or even fourth generation Christians who have been 'born into' families which profess Christianity. While no proper research has been done in this area, we can still make some comments based on certain empirical facts and observations.

We have already mentioned the presence and function of what we call 'diviners' or 'spiritist practitioners'. How such beliefs and practices are immediately relevant to matriliny can be deduced from a few case studies. Some individuals who had adopted their father's name since childhood had gone to the diviners for various needs. The diviners informed them that they could not help them because they had taken their father's clan name. The reason can be traced to the matrilineal lineage and '*ka daw ïng*'. Before diviners can help find a cure they must first trace out the 'cause'. They must be sure that it is a transgression committed by clan members or an external cause. Diagnosing the 'cause' and ensuring the cure involves invoking the help and forgiveness of the clan deity (*ka Leilongkur ka Leilongjait*) and '*Ka Iawbei*'. For this reason one should always use one's mother's clan title.

A Christian who used his father's clan name consulted a diviner, to enquire about the reasons for his failure in business ventures. The 'diviner' informed this person that his father's clan name '*Ka pynjem rngiew*' means life force or personality. The use of father's clan name has weakened and made vulnerable this dynamic personal life force. From that time on, that particular individual has been using his mother's clan name. Again what is worth noting here is that this individual is a professing Christian. He is just one of many practising Christians who have not completely let go of their traditional religious beliefs and practices even though such practices are in direct conflict with Christian teachings. The Old Testament of the Christian Bible explicitly teaches that such practices should be forsaken, and in fact, they are an 'abomination' to the God of the Christians. The organized Christian Church appears to be either unaware or turns a blind eye 'to these practices. Culture and religion are still shrouded in ambiguity. Khasi beliefs appear to be still deeply rooted in Khasi consciousness. Christian teachings have not been fully internalized.

Further, kinship ties, in the final analysis and for the most part are still stronger than congregational ties. Even today, a few Christian converts from non-Christian families face opposition, even the threat of death, from their maternal kinsmen. This is especially so in families where the '*kur*' and the power of the maternal uncles are strong, and in those clans where the converts in question are the youngest daughters, the '*Khadduhs*'.

These few observations on Khasi matriliny today raises such questions as 'what is the future of the Khasi matriliny? Can the system withstand the onslaught of change and exposure to modernizing influences such as education, the communication media, Christianity, or the process of urbanization and technological change? How far has Christian value system been internalized by the Christian Khasis?' We have no definite answers. Further research will throw some light on the above problems.

REFERENCES

1. Johnstone, Ronald, L., *Religion in Society: A Sociology of Religion*, New Jersey, Prentice Hall, 1988.
2. Mawrie, H.O., *Ka Pyrkhat U Khasi*, 1981.
3. Ibid.

6

The Impact of Christianity on the Khasi-Jaintia Matrilineal Family

O.L. Snaitang

The aim of this essay is to examine the influence of Christianity on the Khasi-Jaintia matrilineal family. It will be investigated from an assumption that in the process of changes that have taken place among the Khasi-Jaintia matrilineal people and family in the nineteenth and twentieth centuries, Christianity has contributed to strengthening the matrilineal system. In this connection, we will first of all survey the historical background of the Khasi-Jaintia matrilineal culture before the colonial period. Secondly, the analysis will be on the impact of the British colonial rule upon the people in general and on the family, especially women, in particular. Lastly, this essay will deal with the matrilineal consequences following the arrival of Christianity from the mid-nineteenth century to the present.

Matrilinealism In The Pre-Nineteenth Century

This section will examine the historical context of the Khasi-Jaintia matrilineal system before its interaction with the modern agencies of change in the nineteenth and twentieth centuries. It will deal mainly on matrilinealism, cultural fragmentation and cultural simplicity.

Matrilinealism is a social system which seeks to solidify a given community through sharing of responsibilities based on the process of interiorisation of the content of matrilineal foundation through mother. The Khasi-Jaintia people were a people with no literature but had a number of folk stories on different topics, like, the origin of the race, sin, salvation and with a somewhat less known story on the origin of matrilinealism.[1] The Khasi-Jaintia people were famous hunters; fighters and raiders. Their life was originally primal and isolated with no exposure with the outside world because of thick jungles, distance and fear of demons. They lived a life of instability and kept on moving from one place to another. In the process, the women folk found it difficult to adjust themselves to such a nomadic life. An agreement for a stabilised inhabitation in the interest of women had brought a sigh of relief to mother although it had minimal impact on the unbridled hunting spirit of the men folk who more often than not have no satisfaction in a settled night rest unless they had achieved something through hunting or raiding. While men preferred a moving life of exploring, invading and procreating, women by contrast chose a coherent settled life, even as mere keepers of a home. Their responsibility was greater. They looked after the upbringing of the children, providing food to domesticated animals, cooking, washing and maintaining the family worship intact. They taught the children to know their destiny, to know God and men and to learn the value of righteous dealing in addition to passing on the story of family genealogy to the following generation. In this manner a settled home under the care and supervision of woman was like a school in rudimentary form. Mothers were professors of family religion and law of economic justice.

But men folk who were always on the move did not eventually provide security to the family. They involved themselves in raiding the plains people by looting their belongings, like ornaments, food stuff, domesticated animals and by kidnapping of their women also. Such acts had gradually built anger on the people in the plains who were looking for opportunities to make revenge. In such a situation when Khasi settlement were attacked by plainsmen only women were left at home to defend themselves. Once upon a time, in a rare example of courage, women raised an alarm to all women who together in unity made counter attack against the enemies. In a pitched battle that did not last long, the outsiders were over-powered by the women and some of them were captured alive and kept as captives to be handed over to the men folk when they would be back. But for the captives who had been captured in the fight, the Khasi men could not have believed the account narrated by the women about their exceptional power and victory over the enemies. As a consequence of this incidence, all Khasi men took a unanimous and drastic decision — a decision that has far reaching effect in the people till today, by giving family lineage to mothers as an award in recognition of their exemplary defence and care of the community. Based on a long experience, a decision was also made that the last daughter, who would by the time parents grow old, become physically fit and mentally matured, be made custodian of the family and property alike.

A Khasi-Jaintia family was primarily a family of mother, children and uncles. A father who should be the leading member of the family became less significant because of his role as an uncle on the one hand and the incompatibility of his clan code with that of his wife on the other hand.[2] Whereas his status in the house of his sisters, among his nephews and nieces is supreme, authoritative and decisive, he is nevertheless a mere dummy in the house of his own wife. In the context of the Bhois and Jaintias, a father lives at his mother's house in the day and stays with his wife in the night. He hardly takes anything from his wife's home as his life is bound to his own clan. This system was healthy and suitable as long as the society was in isolation but when it began to get exposed with other living cultures its family foundation appeared shaky.

In a matrilineal society, marriage[3] is a social contract based on clan, religious rites and practices. It is an act performed at the house of a bride in the presence of uncles and brothers from both families, fathers and other invited male members. Marriages in the former days were generally at the direction of the uncles, mothers and in some sections of the society of the fathers also. Adult boys and girls were never given a free choice for marriage especially in the case of girls. It was the elders, especially uncles who initiated the proceedings and made arrangements for boys and girls. At the same time, the society did not believe in early marriage. It is estimated that the most common marriageable age for both boys and girls have been 35 years or above. As before and now, marriage among members of the same clan (*Shi kur*) is a taboo, an incest and a crime. In the same way, sons should not marry cousins who are immediate nieces of their father. History does not have record of dowry or bride price in the society. Because of freedom and openness of both sexes, Khasi-Jaintia society has never brought to book cases of rape. Women's response to the traditional procedure of marriage has been positive because of their over all attachment to children and responsibility for their upbringing. They have kept their promises intact and in most cases have never indulged in any act of violation. For them marriage is an avowed monogamous institution and they never believe in having many husbands. Remarriage is permitted for women but because of such social conscience it can take place only after a period of 12 months of the death of her husband. Any widow who violates this traditional unwritten codes will be frowned upon by both members of her own clan and her husband's clan and by the society as a whole.

A matrilineal society which is governed by uncles and elder brothers has flexible attitude towards sons or men, that is, in terms of marriage. The contrasting feature between men and women was that while the latter preferred a stable life of settlement, the former believed in wandering about. He accepted a stable life with great reluctance. That was apparently the reason why he used to wander beyond the hill region to the plains, kidnapped non-Khasi women, married them and created new clans known subsequently as *Dkhar* or with an easily pronounced *Khar* prefixed to any acceptable name therein. If the complacent spirit of the Khasi women in the ancient past be of any indication, the kidnapped women were mostly placed at the care and supervision of the Khasi mothers.

As stated earlier, though the Khasi-Jaintia matrilineal society has developed a marriage procedure to a somewhat well organised institution, it has nevertheless been in a state of promiscuity. While a woman has strictly followed the sanctity of monogamous marriage, a man has on the contrary, been operating beyond that. He had concubines. This was a normal affair in the ancient matrilineal society — a society with a microscopic population. What a clan needed most was to have as many children, especially daughters, so that it could provide continuity and not face the unfortunate fate of extinction. The kinship code is widened and *ka Mei Kha* (a mother of a husband, literal meaning, a mother who gives birth) recognizes children born from the concubines provided they were brought to her notice in a proper manner and without any violation of clan codes, in addition to those who are born from the original wife. Again, such procedure was healthy in an isolated matrilineal society in antiquity. In an unbelievable development, that is, if we measure by a yardstick of the present setup, a wife, her children, concubines, their children and the respective related clans, not only accepted the phenomenon but even lived amicably and peacefully — a thing that may rarely happen today.

Another factor which had promoted man's promiscuous marriage was the matrilineal lineage itself. A man is attached more to the nephews and nieces than to his children. He has a divided, conflicting and contrasting personality. While as an uncle he commands the sister's family with honour and dignity, as a father he is regarded as a *u khun ki briew* (a son of other persons). In South Jaintia Hill, the family rites cannot be conducted without an uncle (particularly the senior one) but the presence of a man in a capacity as a husband is regarded as an act displeasing to the deities. As a result, the social set up did not make the father to have any responsibility over his children nor did it create in him a sense of belongingness. In a fragmented Khasi- Jaintia culture, the socio-kinship component is the significant factor which helped to bring the entire community to sense of oneness. It brings together members from father's clan and from the mother's clan including those who are in same way interrelated through marriage relations. This aspect is important in the Khasi-Jaintia society because majority of Khasi clans are spread over in the entire Khasi- Jaintia area and so have laid a firm foundation for cultural unity. For instance, the *Laloo* clan in Jaintia hills is related to the *Diengdoh* clan in Khasi hills. Though there may be justification in separating the community through dialects, religious affiliations and political organisation, the closely-knit socio-kinship ties and the clan relations do not in any way rip the integrity of the Khasi-Jaintia cultural solidarity apart. It also contributes to making the people aware of their social interrelatedness so that they will be able to examine whether a marriage is culturally legal or not. In this way, a person can avoid the danger of committing the age-old unforgivable socio-religious crime of incest (*ka shongsang*). That was perhaps one of the reasons why marriage in the distant past was initiated by uncles and elderly persons.

Captivity and Freedom

Though the kinship code has contributed to the larger sense of oneness in a community, nevertheless matrilinealism has over a period of time not done good not only to a man but also to a woman as well. We will here examine the status of a woman and a man. A Khasi-Jaintia woman's status as hypothetically portrayed in the already indicated story above is rather unique because of her exceptional role as a caring mother for a stable family and defender of the community from retaliatory attacks of revenge. Her status in the family and in the society is elevated to a somewhat superior position soon after the imposition of clan lineage and custodianship of family property. As a mother, she is revered as a family goddess. She determines who among her sons would become leader in the clan council or of the state *durbar*. Matriliny has given her a sense of responsibility for the welfare of the children and so she is free to work anywhere including in business transactions in markets in order to make a living for the family. In this connection, the Khasi-Jaintia society does not have instances of female infanticide, dowry or purdah. Even rape was an unknown among the people in antiquity and even in the recent past.

In reality, however, a Khasi-Jaintia woman lived in captivity. Her responsibility for the well-being of the family forced her to work even at the cost of personal sacrifices. A story about *Ka Likai* of *Sohra*[4] was one example of woman's untold sufferings in the matrilineal social structure. In most cases she had to work in the field facing the scorching hot sun or rains even during the period of pregnancy. She was engaged in all sort of works including carrying firewood or water with a suckling baby on. In addition to that she is regarded as a single powered creation *ka kynthei kaba tang shi bor* in the eyes of the male.

A Khasi-Jaintia woman is a born leader but in the context of a matrilineal set up she is everywhere in bondage. She is deprived of leadership rights in all indigenous institutions. Though lineage is traced through a mother, she is not permitted to act as leader or be a member of a clan *durbar.* Provision to the post of rulers from the level of a clan, village, *raid* and upto the state level is reserved to men. Though a rare case of woman-leadership took place at *Nobasohphoh Syiemship* in once upon a time period, that was never an accepted order in the matrilineal system. It was regarded a taboo, at least. Besides that, a woman is excluded from legislative, administrative, judicial and priestly powers. The woman is liberated, but held captive. A man is captive, but is really free. Unlike a woman, a Khasi-Jaintia man is not given rights to family property and lineage, except to a few among the Bangla influenced group of people of the South Khasi-Jaintia Hills. He is the reverse of the status of a woman.[5] A man has home everywhere but nowhere does he live permanently. While a woman's freedom is associated with responsibility of the children's destiny, a man's freedom, in many instances does not bear any responsibility of the wife's family. He plays significant role in the home of his sister in all matters. Suffice it to sum up that matrilinealism sanctions man alone to exercise legislative, administrative, executive, judicial and priestly responsibilities in the community. In order to safeguard this procedure in a matrilineal context, the system warrants further limitation of woman leadership by issuing a well fabricated prophecy of social extinction thus: *wei la kynih ka 'yiar kynthei te ka pyrthei ka la wai'* (once a hen crowed then the world is over).

Cultural Fragmentation

Captivity and freedom are among the most contradictory features in the matrilineal society which have subsequently had impact upon traditional family solidarity. Closely connected with this cultural contradiction had been fragmentation in some elements of the traditional culture. Although an elaboration of this subject is important, nevertheless it is beyond the scope of this investigation. We will therefore deal with two aspects: exclusive leadership and family religion.

We have indicated above that all leading posts in the community were set apart exclusively for men. This was true in polity, legislature, judiciary, administration and priesthood. It however was not meant for all men. Leadership was determined from the particular clan and from the particular mother, for instance, the post of chief (*U Syiem*) of a territorial state. Though a chief must be male, yet not all male members of the society can contest election to that post. It was hereditary and did not make provision for members from other clans. This exclusiveness in the structure of the traditional matrilineal culture did not unfortunately contribute to a sound system of leadership. In short, a pre-nineteenth century leadership was grounded on a limited selective clan sentiments based on a matrilineal succession of sons.

A divided culture among the people was also evident in the traditional religion. In the midst of cultural divisiveness of our people, the word "Khasi Religion"[6] in singular form appeared to have received wide publicity and recognition. There may be some justification if it is used in the plural form. Be that as it may, the only religion ever existed in the traditional Khasi-Jaintia region was a family or a clan religion. Later it developed into a village religion and at most to the level of a single state religion as in *Khyrim, Mylliem* and *Sohra*. Again, the function of a family or a clan religion is from the side of the mother. It is a religion whose legitimate priest is an uncle. Such clan based religion contributes to division in the family. The father, by virtue of belonging to another clan, is completely an outsider to his wife's family religion. While in some areas he may be allowed to contribute materially towards the preparation of the rituals and be present as an onlooker, in *Nongtalang* area of the South Jaintia Hills, a father is not only prohibited from attending family religious worship but is regarded as a taboo if he is inside the family premises as long as the family religious rite of that particular clan is in progress.

Cultural Simplicity

Another feature of the traditional Khasi-Jaintia society in general and the family in particular, was a kind of cultural simplicity. While it is important to touch upon the various dimensions along this line, it is not possible to do justice to them in this paper. Nonetheless we will here refer to two main areas namely, material culture and traditional economy. A traditional life of the Khasi-Jaintia family was on the whole primal because of its isolation, fragmentation and exclusiveness. As to this component — the material culture[7] of the Pre-British hill people, we will try to do it in a general way touching at least on some significant elements.

Let us start with a residential house first. A house of the Khasi people was built in such a way as to look almost exactly like a shape of a turned upside down boat. It was small in size, short, unspacious with no proper ventilation. There were no separate rooms. It was covered with thatched grass. Chairs, tables and even cots or mattresses were apparently not known in the early period of antiquity. People did not know the art of decoration as the interior remained almost dark even in the day time. Cooking materials were limited. There were a few plates, cups, bamboo pitcher for drawing water and earthen pots or jars. Food items were also very simple. They included mostly meat, dried fish, salt, vegetables, and a little quantity of rice which was cooked together with tapioca flour etc. Home made rice beer was in most cases daily drinks and was served even to children.

The simplicity of the traditional culture was also evident in the dresses of both women and men. While most men hardly washed in many weeks specially in cold winter months, women appeared to be content with the application of inexpensive simple cosmetics, like fat of animals or fruit juice. Mirrors, variety of soaps, perfumes, modern cosmetics and other complex dressing items had not found easy way to the ancient family. Cleanliness in the house and its surroundings was an unknown art. Hence, the compound which lacked drainage system, was filled with all sorts of domesticated animals. As a consequence of such unhealthy environment, people in the family most often than not, fell prey to various diseases. The simple Khasi people attribute the cause of all ailments to demons. Cholera, malaria and other dreaded diseases were perceived by the people as some personified creatures. Unhygienic life had generally led to high infant mortality rate especially in the northern *Bhoi* region.[8]

The economic dimension[9] was another area of primal innocence of the people. Goods were exchanged and not bought. Counting was very simple. While originally the people could count at most upto 30, in due course they could develop their counting ability upto less than a thousand. They also adopted simple weighing and measuring systems. Days of a week were called by the names of markets, and, to the traditional calendar of the people, there were eight days in a week. Shops in markets were temporarily built for protection from heavy rainfall in summer. Most dealers spread selling materials openly on the ground and engaged in this manner for two times in eight days in the same market place. Hence people normally exchanged essential commodities that would last until the next market day.

Cultural Consequences of the Imposition of the New Government[10]

The Khasi-Jaintia primal world of isolation, difference, divisiveness, exclusiveness and simplicity, was dashed after the imposition of a new government — the British, in the early part of the nineteenth century. There were three main reasons why the British entered upon the affairs of the region: they wanted to construct road communication between the plains of the southern Bangla and Assam, to contain the formidable raiding of the Khasis upon the plain areas and to build sanatoria because of healthy environment compared to the malaria-affected plains.

The advent of the British powers has tumbled down the traditional defences of the Khasi-Jaintia people. The isolation of the region was for the first time broken down and brought it to the larger exposure with the outside world. After subduing some of the Khasi chiefs who resisted through some form of warfare and demolishing the traditional Syiemship rule of the *Sutnga* state in 1835, the first thing that the British did was to enter into treaty agreement. Then, they consolidated the erstwhile fragmented territorial states under one administration, the British (though they divided the area into two distinct parts, states and non-states).

The introduction of a new administration has ushered a new era among the people. The entire area which was formerly independent and subjected to no outside empires, was now tagged on to the larger British map. The system of government that was imposed among the matrilineal culture has opened up a new work culture. The procedure of appointment was now done on the basis of qualification and not on muscle power. In the context of the matrilineal male dominated leadership, the introduction of the British administration has come as a good news to women. The freedom given to woman in the early period of British settlement was significant and served as a foundation for women leadership in the subsequent century and well into the present. Nevertheless, it brought a cultural crisis. The people could not adjust themselves to such traumatic change in a new set-up.

In the absence of well qualified indigenous personnel, the British authority appointed outsiders to work as clerks, technical workers, engineers, labourers and military chaplains. The presence of these outsiders added further crisis to the primal isolated society. In addition to that they also imposed legal rules and conduct. The creation of cantonment with well-equipped military personnel, arms and magazines had deeply affected the morale of the people and caused a cultural trauma. The construction of office buildings and residential quarters on a new architectural style has also overshadowed the traditional thatched houses.

The new culture was also evident in the introduction of cots, sleeping materials, curtains, chairs, tables, almirah, mirrors and other interior decorations. The simplicity of indigenous earthen goods was now shattered with the availability of steel, ceramic crockery, cutlery and drinking glasses of various kinds. Further, the British initiated modern dresses, a variety of cosmetics, soaps, tooth-paste and brush, clothing materials, pants, shirts, blouses, shoes and other modern life styles. While all these features have considerable influence upon the people and brought crisis of adjustment, they have also shaped the traditional family. This new culture began to make both wife and husband bear similar responsibility for a common development of the family. It was apparently the beginning of a shift of emphasis from the responsibility of an uncle to a father.

Another area that was greatly affected was the traditional economy. The primal barter economy was now in the process of crumbling following the introduction of money economy. The British officials also brought ration goods, oil, kerosene oil, lantern and finished iron products. The imposition of a new calendar year counting seven days in a week, had tremendous impact on the traditional eight days a week. The simplicity of the traditional selling of goods in markets was complicated with the addition of new cooking, dressing and building materials. Modern weighing system and measures began to displace the barter economy completely.

The imposition of a wide technological communication like, radio, wireless, post and telegraphs; motor transport, ropeway, cinemas, and other systems contributed to further intensifying crisis in the society and the family as well. And as already indicated above, such developmental institutions warranted appointment of outsiders. The presence of these British or plains people, subsequently led to inter-marriage between them and the Khasi-Jaintia women. As a result, one witnessed the rise of the British named clans with some indication of patrilineal pattern. What the people needed most was education of children so that they can adjust themselves successfully in a British administered world.

One can go on spelling out these new elements that have been introduced in the region but suffice it to enunciate that the British government was the main agency for the major change in the traditional family clan-based society. While these new elements broke down people's age old isolation and opened up avenues for women's liberation in modern institutions, they were by contrast not in a position to function effectively and so faced a trauma that might in the long run lead to detribalisation.[11] It was in such situation that Christianity came in and participated in the changing process.

The Impact of Christianity on the Khasi-Jaintia Matrilineal Family

In the midst of cultural trauma that has happened among the people after the advent of the British authority, Christianity took part in the process by introducing a number of developmental projects which made the people to successfully adjust and function themselves in a changing situation.

The first ever Christian missionary who has initiated work of evangelisation of the Khasis (at Pandua, now in Bangladesh, of the former *Sohra Syiemship)* was none other than the famous Serampore Baptist Mission Bengali convert, Rev. Krishna Chandra Pal. Though the Mission extended missionary work among the people under the supervision of colonoial rulers resident at Sylhet, it however withdrew itself completely from the region in 1838 immediately after its merger with the original Baptist Missionary Society. The gap was subsequently filled by the Welsh Calvinstic Methodist Mission in 1841. Unlike the colonially backed Serampore Mision, the Welsh Mission entered upon the activities of the poeple without any connection with the British Government. It was the Mission that had contributed immensely towards the development of the Khasi-Jaintia people. The Catholic Mission which has come 50 years later, in 1890, has made tremendous contribution to the entire society specially in higher educational field. Other foreign Missions in the region have been, the Church of England (today CNI), the seventh Day Adventists, Pentecostal Mission and others. And Churches formed by the Khasi-Jaintia people themselves in the 20th century which participated in the larger process of acculturation, have been and Church of God, the Christ .National Church, All One-In-Christ Church Fellowship, Church of Jesus Christ-Full Gospel and other groups. In addition to these Missions and Churches of indigenous origins, there have been ecumenical organisations as well.

A brief examination of the attitude of the Christian missionaries towards the Khasi-Jaintia matrilineal culture is important so that one can understand the Christian impact on the matrilineal family. The word culture is used here in a sense that it is an ongoing process of life of a community whose struggle for separate identities involves political, religious, linguistic, social and material components. In the Khasi-Jaintia context, all these elements are well-knit together almost in a single territorial state, *Ka hima*. If one cmponent is affected the entire cultural fabric will be shaken.

The Christian missionaries, particularly the Welsh, who hailed from a predominantly patriarchal society were puzzled by their contacts with a matrilineal people in which women were not subjected to ill-treatment and subjugation. However, the fact that they (i.e. the Welsh missionaries) themselves were originally of low class background and had passed through periods of exploitation and discrimination at the hands of the advanced and wealthy English elites, realised how sensitive it was if the fundamental cultural components were overlooked. Closely associated with this understanding was their commitment that they have come over to the isolated hill region with a specific evangelical mission, that is, to preach the good news of salvation through Jesus Christ. Hence, their attitude towards the Khasi-Jaintia culture was complex because while they advocated maintaining the status quo, i.e., the matrilineal system, they minced no words in rejecting the traditional religious component in a Christian community.

The exclusive evangelical faith of Christian missions, especially those from the Protestant traditions, has made the indigenous converts to renounce outright the traditional religious components. The substitution with the new faith, practice and structure has however not displaced the indigenous social bond, rather it helped perpetuating a common sense of identity from the level of a clan to the level of an entire community. They have also not denounced the kinship institution and the matrilineal system. Converts still retained their family name, system of inheritance, clan durbar, representation at the traditional state Assembly and even chieftainship. While intra-clan marriage was prohibited in a Christian community, a sin of incest (*ka shongsang*) is still regarded as a crime. In order to help propagate its seriousness in a Christian church, the Welsh Mission has created a special vigilance committee — The Standing Incest Committee with members from the indegenous Christians in addition to the missionaries.

In the context of changes that have occurred among the Khasi-Jaintia people of the present Meghalaya, Christianity even without any fore-knowledge of such traumatic change, has provided a variety of institutions that have appropriately served the specific needs of the people for successful adjustment and progress. The most significant of these institutions have been: the universalisation of a single language for the whole tribe; introduction of Latin alphabet and literature; establishment of a wide educational school network and boarding houses; health services; ecclesiastical organisation and theology. These Christian developmental components have far reaching effect upon the erstwhile isolated, fragmented, exclusive and simplistic society and contributed to creating a solidified community. They have also shaped the society not only to get going with the new set-up but to be able to resist major crisis. In this respect, the role of education is worth mentioning. It taught the people arithmetic, elementary science, English and other subjects. These attempts have in due course made the people knowledgeable about money economy; weights and measures, communication through English and some knowledge about technology in addition to cementing a feeling of common social heritage.

Christianity has, however, not encouraged women leadership except in the field of school education and health service. In this connection, Christianity had apparently adopted the traditional system where women were deprived of leadership rights in all indigenous decision making bodies. With an exception of the Church of Jesus Christ-Full Gospel, other Churches have not encouraged induction of women to the ordained ministry. Women are still relegated to a somewhat subordinate position. Even in a much advanced Khasi-Jaintia Presbyterian Synod, the Ministry of full time executive women affairs is headed not by a woman but by a man. Women are reduced to a level of 'workers'. In most churches the task of women's association or committee has been to collect funds for male-governed churches or institutions. But for the provision of the British system of government which was continued in the post-independent India. Khasi-Jaintia women would not have an iota of liberation and joy in any legislative, administrative, executive and judicial posts. Nevertheless,

Christianity has provided means for successful women leadership in institutions outside the ordained ministry.

The contention that Christianity has approved the traditional matriliny of the Khasi-Jaintia people should in no way give the impression that its social system needed no change. And Christianity while defending the matrilineal structure in a Christian community, also sought to modify some of its unhealthy elements for a more solidified family. We will now here concentrate its impact on marriage, family and kinship.

Matrilinealism has approved monogamous marriage among women and polygamy among men. Going by a yard stick of today's culture, our immediate reaction to such discrepancy would be social inequality, injustice and discrimination to women. While there may, no doubt, be some truth in it, nevertheless it is not so because a women's monogamy and man's polygamy have from the ancient past received approval not only from uncles but from mothers as well. Christian missionaries introduced ecclesiastical law code which while approving monogamous marraige alone in a Christian Community, it disapproved any promiscuous act, polygamy, polyandry or extra-marital contacts. Converts who commit any of such acts would consequently be excommunicated. Laws of suspension or excommunication are applicable even to unmarried converts if they indulge in sexual relations before the regular marriage procedure is approved and enacted. Hence, whereas the matrilineal marriage is maintained, the modification in the imbalanced marriage structure through church rules has at least contributed to the strenghtening of a matrilineal family.

Divorce was another significant feature which had weakened traditional family. It was a common phenomenon in the society because the flexible and mixed matrilineal marriage system could be declared null and void through simple symbolic act and pronouncements either by a man or a woman or both.[12] The impact of Christian teaching on this aspect is therefore important, although its effectiveness in a society with long history of marriage flexibility is never satisfactory. The sanctity of Christian marriage (the Catholics regarded it as a holy sacrament) is urther strengthened by the imposition of the Indian Christian Marriage Act within most of the

Protestant Churches. While this act makes provision for divorce, it is nonetheless not as simple as in the traditional set-up. This was the reason why Christian marriage in Khasi-Jaintia hills is never brought within the ambit of the unrecorded customary laws or conventions because once this traditional divorced procedure is approved in a Christian community it will never be possible to curb its subsequent pervasiveness even if the Church wants to forbid it.

Christian marriage was both a civil and religious institution. It places importance upon unity, peace and mutual understanding from both the parties, from the society and from the Church. The strength of this institution is, therefore, seen in a well defined combination of a clan (uncles, mothers and elder brothers or sisters), a father's clan (father, father's, mother and the elders), a Church (pastor, deacons, elders and members) and a government act. In this process each component is inter-related and has its own part to contribute to the body of the marriage institution and all are important and necessary.

The Protestant teaching on a person's private reasoning or judgement in matters of faith has considerable influence on traditional decision for marriage. Earlier elders initiated the marriage for their sons/nephews or daughters/nieces and most children married late in years. Today most children from Christian communities or even those from indigenous organisations make decision of their own in selecting partners, going for courtship and getting married even in thier teens.

Modernization (British rule and Christianity) has brought about changes in the traditional society. Its contribution to strengthening matrilineal family has the consequence of creating at least more responsibility on the parents and lessening the responsibility of uncles. This change has, however, not shaken the matrilineal system. In other words, while the immediate and major responsibility of a father is now with his wife, and children, his role as an uncle in his sisters's house is still significant, though not with the same authority as he used to enjoy before. In today's context a husband (or a father) invests almost everything with his wife and children (expect his clan's name, of course) and hardly makes substantial material investment with his sister's home. Again, the gap in her home is now filled by a husband/a father. This shift of responsibility from uncles to fathers was in most cases promoted by the Christian missonaries. For instance, a Welsh missionary, Rev. Jerman Jones who worked among the Jaintias, encouraged a solidified parental family instead of a traditional clan-based visiting husband. His proposal has worked out well in today's Jaintia society as a whole. In this process, a change in the status of uncle and father has not brought any cultural imbalance, rather empowered the matrilineal family structure. Apparently in no other period of the people's history have children recieved more parental attention than it has now, at least after the gradual ushering in of a dynamic life-style since the first half of the nineteenth century and subsequently well even into the twentieth. The missionaries' concern for encouraging a parental family has a religious motive behind it. That is, parents should lead family prayers and Bible reading, bring up the children in a Christian atmosphere, and take them to church service and Sunday schools. At the time of Baptism or dedication of children, it is the parents who make vows publicly to the priest and the congregation committing themselves to provide proper Christian nurture and development to the children. As of today, the parents alone take care of the children's education from the primary level and upto the level of college or university degree education either at their own home town or outside the region. Therefore, though the promotion of a parental responsibility for the growth of the children in the Khasi-Jaintia matrilineal society has been mainly due to the religious interests of the missonaries, it has in due course tremendous effect on the society as a whole, i.e., it strengthened the family solidarity. Closely associated with this is the policy of the goverment in providing a column of father's name which is compulsory for all official applications but not that of either uncle's or mother's name.

Conclusion

We have come to the concluding section of our study. We have seen how the isolated Khasi-Jaintia society was disturbed following the intrusion of the mighty imperialists in the early part of the nineteenth century. In the context of cultural incapacitation, Christianity which has played a secondary participation agent of·change has helped in creating a new cultural set up. Because of its soft attitude towards the traditional matriliny and kinship ties, the long cherished matrilinealism is retained and the modification of some imbalanced elements in it have in due course laid a foundation for a continuing matrilineal culture. Notwithstanding the facts that we have demonstrated thus far, the burning question which should draw our reflection today is; how far, has matrinilinealism been constructive, creative or helpful, not only to man but also to woman as well, in the context of constant pressure from the predominant patriarchal cultural onslaught in almost in all walks of life?

NOTES AND REFERENCES

1. There are still other folk stories about the origin of matrilinealism among the khasi-Jaintia people. While almost all of them have similar acounts with a slightly different events, they are nevertheless reaching the same conclusion. One of such stories is worth mentioning as under:

   Once upon a time in a pitched battle that had claimed most of the lives of Khasi warriors, a lone Khasi survivor who had to fight the last battle knew not for sure of his survival to provide continuity to the community, so he finally handed over the clan lineage to his mother and made her custodian of property as well.
2. See Kelian Synrem, "Ka bynta U Rangbah kum U Kni bad kum U Kpa", in Ba Ioh Ngi Klet Shillong: 1994 pp. 26–35.
3. P.R.T. Gurdon, The Khasis, originally published 1907, reprinted 1975, pp. 127ff.
4. Mrs. Rafy, Khasi Folk Tales, (First published 1920, reprinted 1985), pp. 85–88.
5. For an exemplified study of a status of man from a khasi woman's perspective, see Kelian Synrem, op. cit., pp. 26ff.
6. A rather less inclusive but detailed study of the Khasi religion has been written by Dr. H. Lyngdoh Nonglait, Ka Niam Khasi, Shillong: First published 1937, reprinted 1970.
7. See Frederick S. Downs, *Christianity in North East India: Historical Perspectives*, Delhi: 1983.
8. R.A Huges, "Ka Mission Jingpynkhiah Ka Synod" in Ki Khubor Jong Ki Jing-iaseng Jubilee 1841–1966, 1967, pp. 1–15.
9. U. Donrai, Ka History Shaphang Ka Jingwallam Nyngkong eh Ka Niam Khristan ha kane Ka Ri Khasi Jaintia da Ka Welsh Calvinistic Methodist Mission, First published 1914, revised and reprinted by O.D Laitphlang, 1956, p. 99.

10. For further information, see David' R. Syiemlieh, *British Administration in Meghalaya: Policy and Pattern*, New Delhi: 1989.
11. O.L. Snaitang, *Christianity and Social Change in Northeast India* 1993, pp. 140 ff.
12. Gurdon, op. cit., 79 ff.

7

Changes in the Matrilineal System of Khasi-Jaintia Family

Philomath Passah

The Khasis, the Jaintias and the Garos of Meghalaya were considered to be matriarchal societies where a woman or a mother was supposed to be the head of the family. But these tribes refuse to accept that their societies are truly matriarchal. Though descent is reckoned through the female line, yet man is the head of a family among them. Hence the three societies are not matriarchal but are matrilineal where descent is based on the mother or the female line while the family headship belongs to the males. However this paper is an attempt to recount a number of changes that have gradually taken place in the matrilineal system of the Khasi-Jaintia family.

Roles of the Youngest Daughter and the Maternal Uncle

The matrilineal system of the Khasi-Jaintia family is a system in which descent is based on the female line but the family property is under the control and supervision of the uncles and/or the brothers. The tribes did not have any traditional law of inheritance. The customary right or the right to property in the strictly legal sense was not in vogue among them. It may be wrong to think that their custom had ever conferred on the youngest daughter the right of a legal heir. According to their custom, the youngest daughter is only the custodian of the properties which should be managed and controlled by her maternal uncles and on their death, by her brothers. The youngest daughter has of course a number of duties and privileges and "the youngest daughter of each family in each generation succeeded to the office of custodianship over family property and religion."[1]

Thus the youngest daughter is herself an institution and among the Jaintias, the ancestral home where she lives to take charge of the family wealth and property is treated as God's house (*I Yung blai*). The duties of the youngest daughter as the custodian are fairly heavy. She has to assist her maternal uncle in the performance of religious rites and holding of ceremonies in *I Yung blai* and to meet all the expenses for them. She should allow the body of a dead relative to remain in the house until taken for cremation. She receives the bones or the ashes of those who died and cremated elsewhere far away from home before the same are kept in the family cairn (tombstones) during a ritual ceremony known as *I Rah Chyien* (shifting of bones from the place of death to the native place) among the Jaintias. She has to allow all ceremonies like wedding, naming and all other religious rites being held in her ancestral house. Besides she has to look after any members of the family or her kin group who might have fallen into misfortune due to disability, death of a husband or wife, divorce and so on.

Though the youngest daughter is a custodian of the family properties, yet she has no absolute authority over them. She could not sell or dispose of any part of them. For the purpose of disposing any family property — land or other movable or immovable properties — it is the family council consisting of the maternal uncles and brothers of the youngest daughter, which should decide and give consent to her. The eldest maternal uncle who should preside over the discussion, has in fact the final say in the matter.

A maternal uncle in the Khasi-Jaintia custom used to occupy a pride of place in a family or a kinship group. He exercises control over the management of the properties — movable and immovable — of the family. Thus "authority and control are in the hands of the maternal uncles."[2] He acts as the true representative of the family or kin group. Among the traditional Jaintias in particular, the husband is like a stranger in his wife's house and can hardly interfere in the family matters of her clan. It is his brothers-in-law and the uncles of the wife who play the vital role in his wife's kin group affairs. The husband only visits his wife at night and generally leaves her house at dawn. But among the educated and the Christian families, a change has now taken place where the husband becomes part of his wife's family and has tended to neglect his maternal house and properties by letting his youngest sister and her husband the freedom to manage the ancestral property as they like.

Changing Role of Youngest Daughter and Maternal Uncle

The changes have also taken place whereby the youngest daughter can make a claim to the family properties as a legal heir. This change was facilitated during the British rule when wrong interpretation of the local custom was made by courts and lawyers who did not understand the language and depended much upon interpreters whose own knowledge of the language was also faulty.[3] This has greatly helped the youngest daughter to successfully manipulate and treat the properties, ancestral or otherwise, as personal or self-acquired and dispose them as she pleases.[4] She could even grab all properties of her parents and grand-parents for her sole benefit.

While the power of the youngest daughter has thus increased beyond custodianship, the customary role and power of the maternal uncle has declined beyond measure. His role has now become, in general, mournfully insignificant.

Organized Attempts for Change

As education came and spread among the tribes, the efficacy of the matrilineal system of descent and inheritance began to be questioned. Right from the beginning of the present century, serious concerns had been raised by those among the elite group.[5] This concern has been intensified during the last 30 years or more. The views of many people, young and old, men and women, have constantly been expressed regarding the merits and demerits of the traditional system through the language newspapers and booklets. Many write-ups pleading for a change-over to the patrilineal system have been published from time to time.

In 1961, an organization by the name of *Ka Seng Iktiar Longbriew Manbriew* was formed in Khasi Hills to spearhead a movement for a change in the system. Its members comprised both Khasis and Jaintias. Its constitution provided for a radical change both in descent and rights of succession and inheritance. But it could not make much headway. At some stage a section of the members of the organization wanted a mere change in the right of inheritance.[6] The movement continued since then. It may be mentioned that a practice has already started in some part of Khasi Hills whereby the sons also inherit properties. Among the War Khasis in the Shella confederacy and the adjoining villages, both boys and girls inherit property. Among the Jaintias, the sons can jointly inherit the properties of their parents who have no daughter.

The erstwhile United Khasi-Jaintia Hills Autonomous District Council, appreciating the persistent movement for a change that had continued for quite some time though in a subdued note, decided to introduce the will system among the Khasis-Jaintias empowering the parents to bequeath their self-acquired properties to whomsoever they wish. The parents would then be enabled to gift their self-acquired property either to a daughter or a son or to distribute it among both daughters and sons.

A Bill was accordingly drafted and widely circulated but it was not passed by the District Council. Subsequently in 1980, that is, long after Jaintia Hills got its own separate autonomous district council, the Bill was reactivated and passed. But the Act did not receive the assent of the Governor. The State Government suddenly took interest in the matter and requested its Law Commission to study the case and to draft a fresh and suitable Bill. Obviously, the then Meghalaya State Government was interested in introducing a system of inheritance for the first time in the matrilineal family of the Khasis-Jaintias. The Law Commission subsequently submitted its report with a draft Bill providing necessary powers to enable the Khasi-Jaintia parents to bequeath their self-acquired properties through a will to any of their daughters or sons.

The Bill was duly passed by the Meghalaya Legislative Assembly as the "The Meghalaya Succession to Self-Acquired Property (Khasi and Jaintia Special Provision) Act 1984" which received the assent of the President of India in 1986. The Act does not extend throughout Meghalaya thus excluding the Garos from its application.

The Meghalaya Act 1984 does not apply to the ancestral properties. Its provisions to enable the parents to dispose of their self-acquired properties by a will would suffice and should have satisfied all those who pleaded for a change-over to the patrilineal system. But they have not. The movement has not subsided but persisted. On the 14th of April 1990, a new organization called the Syngkhong Rympei Thymmai was launched to further intensify the movement. The new organization thus replaces the erstwhile Ka Seng Iktiar Longbriew Manwbriew and has presently spread and expanded its membership among the Khasi and Jaintias in Khasi Hills. But it has yet to extend its activities to Jaintia Hills. The sole objective of the organization according to its constitution is to bring about a change into a full-fledged patrilineal system. The members of the organization have reasons to feel aggrieved as the State Government of Meghalaya has failed to bring the Meghalaya Act 1984 into force by a notification. The Act has by now become a dead letter in the absence of a government formal notification to give effect to its application. Unlike the Malabar Marriage Act of 1896 which led to the reform of the Nair's ancient matrilineal joint family system,[7] the Meghalaya Act 1984 had failed to become a progressive legislation. The Meghalaya Act was nothing but a still-born baby.

NOTES AND REFERENCES

1. Juanita War, "Status of Women in Traditional Khasi Culture" in Soumen Sen (ed.) *Women in Meghalaya*, Daya Publishing House, Delhi, 1992, p. 15.
2. I.M. Syiem, *Women in Meghalaya*, op. cit., p. 23.
3. *Report of the Land Reforms Commission for Khasi Hills*, Shillong, 30th November, 1974, p. 35; also, R.T. Rymbai, "Laws and Customs of the Jaintias" in The Implanter, Vol. IV, No. 48, Shillong, September 3, 1972.
4. H. Bareh, *The History and Culture of the Khasi People*, p. 338.

5. See "*U Khasi Mynta*", June 1901 and August 1901; also "*U Lurshai*", June 1914 and September 1916. All cited in the *Report of the Land Reforms Commission for Khasi Hills.*
6. P.M. Passah, "Inheritance Among Matrilineal Tribes of North-Eastern Region of India: Its Socio-Economic Implications and Evolution" in *Vision*, Journal of the Institute of Economics and Social Studies, Bhubaneswar, Vol. VII, No. 3&4, January–June 1988.
7. "Fall in Kerala's Ancient Matrilineal System" in *The Assam Tribune*, March 9, 1994.

8

Some Aspects of Change in the Family System of the Khasis

Aldila Mawlong

One of the most fascinating areas of study in any society has been social change, that is, the study of the conditions under which the disruption of the old traditional order of society has occurred, and the conditions which have led to the explosive emergence of a new 'era'. This transformation of men and social systems is necessitated by numerous factors, which can be broadly classified into social, political and economic factors.

The Khasi people as a society have reached that point of time where a need is felt for a serious re-examination and re-evaluation of institutions, laws and cherished customs, and their use and relevance in the present day context. The advent of Christianity and the forces of modernization in Khasi society have undoubtedly weakened the matrilineal system, which forms the core of the Khasi social structure.

It should be pointed out from the outset that the family system of the Khasis is inextricably connected with the principle of matriliny. Ways of tracing descent, property issues, role of the father vis-a-vis the maternal uncle, role of the female child as compared to the male, are issues related, both to the understanding of Khasi matriliny in general and the Khasi family system in particular.

The Khasi has come a long way from the traditional agricultural society to that of the modern urbanized society.

Many Khasi people are holding blue-collared as well as white-collared jobs far removed from the traditional agrarian setting. Are the customs and traditions which were evolved to suit an agrarian based society still relevant? Has modernization weakened or strengthened the matrilineal system?

The topic is in fact a burning issue; seminars and discussions have been organised to analyse the relevance of matriliny. Issues such as nomenclature, property and authority distribution are debated, be it in tea-stalls or seminar halls. Legislations such as the Meghalaya Succession to Self-Acquired Property Act 1984 has further added fuel to flames. Today, the *Syngkhong Rympei Thymmai* (an association aimed at bringing about changes in the present matrilineal society) has extended to the rural areas; their success, however, is yet to be gauged.

Impact of Modernization

The biggest impact on the Khasi social structure came with the British annexation of the Khasi Hills (1833) followed by the Jaintia Hills (1835). With these annexations, the process of transformation of a small isolated community began. Prior to British annexation, the Khasis had been successful in retaining social and political exclusiveness in spite of the influence of the people from the neighbouring plains. Commercial relations with the plains did provide important routes of cultural exchange as the Jaintias bear a testimony of Hindu influences. However the kind of change brought in by the British is incomparable. The British introduced a new system of administration, better forms of transport and communication, and other infrastructural and paraphernalia of a modern society. Two things, however, stand out distinctly — Christianity and Modernization.

The British paved the way for missionary activities particularly the Welsh Calvinist Methodist who set up their mission in the Hills in 1841. The missionaries introduced a written script, male and female education, vocational skills and health care. Thus with the advent of Christianity, and modern education, a transformation took place in the social and cultural life of the people. For instance, Christianity preached the sanctity of a conjugal life, and the moral duties of the parents towards their children. This indirectly resulted in greater importance given to nuclear families consisting of husband, wife and children. Christianity also stressed on the sanctity of marriage.

With the conversion to Christianity, the institution of *Ka Khadduh* which is closely connected to the Khasi religion has lost its true meaning in the present day context. Christians today no longer observe the rituals connected with Khasi religion. Ceremonies related to the return of the bones of a man to his clan ossuary does not apply to Christians. Christian Khasis bury their dead according to Christian rituals and beliefs, in a common cemetry. From these one may agree that some kinship practices, so closely allied to religion have altered or been forsaken.

The process of education and the impact of the west brought in a new educated middle class who played a vital role in the process of cultural revivalism. The Seng Khasi movement emerged as a retaliation against the total erosion of Khasi culture and religion. This cultural awakening found expression through a literary movement initiated by Babu Jeebon Roy who may be regarded as the apostle of the Khasi renaissance, leading to the establishment of the Seng-Khasi at Mawkhar, Shillong.

The term modernization implies a widespread change and transformation of the societies. The main factors of modernization are education, industrialization, urbanization, literary and mass communication. The process may take various paths; some customs and values may undergo changes while some may aid the process of modernization by carrying forward the past tradition and bringing about a new pattern and a fresh combination. Modernization, and all that goes with it, has played a key role in changing ways of thinking and acting. Urbanization has brought about diverse cultural interactions and different ways of life. The mixing of various cultural patterns leads to assimilation and produces what Louis Wirth[1] termed a 'Mass Urban Culture' in his influential paper "Urbanism as a Way of Life". The quest for better education, jobs and a better way of life has resulted in rural migration to urban centres. Shillong has borne the brunt of this and today faces all the complexities of urbanization.

One of the major consequences of urbanization and migration has been the disintegration of the *Kpoh*. The controlling authority vested on the maternal uncle has become ineffective or has altered to a large extent. As quoted in *U Lurshai* "when a man insures his life, now he makes his children the beneficiaries, not his nephews and nieces. The father is tired of being an uncle, he has seen that it suits him better to be a father than to be an uncle, also for it has been found that double role works no more."[2]

Modern education and new occupations have brought forth a new class of professionals, bureaucrats and technocrats. Both Khasi men and women have benefited from it. As a result of this, a large number of Khasi men and women are holding responsible and competent jobs. This new sense of independence must be in constant conflict with clan solidarity, as cohesion of the clan which primarily centred around the land has naturally disintegrated. As stated by the Japanese Anthropologist, Chie Nakane,[3] the Khasi social organization is a unique example of the functional atomization which reduces the clan merely to regulating selection of spouses and defining the matrilineal identity of a person. The most important corporate functional unit is the *iing* or household comprising of a generation depth of two to four.

Desirability of Change in Matriliny

Education has not just brought about a conflict in the role of authority between father and brother-in-law, but has resulted in the questioning of the relevance and necessity of some of the practices associated with matriliny. The *Syngkhong Rympei Thymmai* (Association of new hearths) is an example of the above. It is a radical movement. According to this organization, the ills of present day Khasi society can be traced to its matrilineal character. Illegitimacy, irresponsibility of the Khasi men to take their family duties seriously in particular and their careless life in general, are caused by the system. The cure, according to them would lie in complete transformation from a matrilineal system to a patrilineal one. The objectives of the association have been outlined in a booklet.[4] However, the solutions stated in the booklet appear vague and prejudicial, leaning towards male-bias.

The two main streams of thought with regard to the debate of matriliny/patriliny issues are the pro-changers led by the organization *Ka Syngkhong Rympei Thymmai* and the moderates. The first represents revolutionary changes while the second represents changes with caution. The latter group is convinced that social problems can be tackled by other means which do not necessarily touch the lineage issue. Economic issues such as inheritance patterns do not come in conflict with descent patterns. The system is flexible enough to tackle economic issues without harming the kinship and descent patterns.

The current paper aims at studying the trends that are emerging with regard to the family system amongst the urban Khasis. Owing to the nature of the study — that is, the need to study changes in a comparatively homogenous population, the localities of Mawkhar and Jaiaw in Shillong were chosen as models of a Khasi urban community. Both these areas have a predominantly Khasi population and have been the seat of cultural revivalism, education and Christian proselytisation.

Both Jaiaw and Mawkhar are located in the western part of Shillong. Both are tribal inhabited areas with negligible presence of non-tribals. The fieldwork was done in the year 1994. A total number of eighty respondents, forty men and forty women, were interviewed by the author with the help of an interview schedule. Initially it was planned that both the husband and wife of the same family would be interviewed. However, this proved impossible due to lack of cooperation. The electoral roll was used as a way of choosing the respondents. As per the electoral rolls, Jaiaw has 718 households and Mawkhar has 143 households. Each individual who was selected was married and out of forty married women, fifteen were *Khadduhs.* The majority of the interviewees were Christians. The respondents varied from age of twenty-six to sixty years. They came from varied occupational background (see Table 1) such as doctors, bank employees, engineers and government employees. Their income varied considerably. Nine individuals reported the lowest income, Rs. 2000 to Rs. 3999

Table 1: Occupations of the Respondents

Occupation	Male %	Female %
Government Service	32.5	25.0
Doctors	17.5	10.0
Engineers	12.5	5.0
Business	15.0	10.0
Bank Employees	7.5	5.0
Teachers	5.0	30.0
Pastors	5.0	0.0
Advocates	2.5	0.0
Politicians	2.5	2.5
Housewife	0.0	12.5
Total	100.0	100.0

per month. Thirty-nine respondents acknowledged income between Rs. 4000 to Rs. 6999 per month. Thirteen interviewees said that they had a monthly income of above Rs. 10,000 and one of them had income above Rs. 18,000 per month. The rest reported income varying from Rs. 7000 to Rs. 9999.

Contrary to popular belief, the father is the head of the household (*U kpa u khlieh ka ïng*). He is respected and loved by his children and in his old age he is looked after by his daughter. If he, due to certain circumstances, is forced to return to his natal home, it would be a matter of shame not only to him as a man and provider, but also to his children who have not been able to honour the basic rules of conduct *tip-kur tip-kha*. Most of the fathers look towards their children for security in their old age.

Table 2 points out the opinion of both male and female respondents, regarding the head of household. This is a highly controversial issue in matrilineal societies. A study of responses brings forth an interesting picture. Ninety, per cent of the male respondents and 80 per cent of the female respondents point out that the *husband* should be the head of household. Ten per cent of the male respondents (who are incidentally married to *Khadduhs*) state that their *father-in-law* should be the head and *not* the mother-in-law. The economic capacity of the father naturally plays a vital role. An able provider is

Table 2: Views regarding Head of Household

Head of Household should be	Views of Men %	Views of Women %
Husband	90	80
Wife's father	10	12.5
Wife's mother	0	7.5
	100.00	100.0

respected not only by his family but his wife's matrikin too. On many occasions, he is given the honour of playing a vital role in decision making in his in-law's household.

Chie Nakane's indepth study on the Khasi matriliny has proved to be both enlightening and relevant. She has studied the status and role of husbands and wives by dividing men into those married to an heiress and those married to non-heiress. Her findings show that those marriages between a man with a non-heiress are more successful, and conjugal ties are stronger. "The domestic residential unit is an elementary family. From the outset of the marriage, the husband's labour is of great importance to his family, since a non-heiress usually has no economic background . . . A man who succeeds at the beginning of his married life is respected and honoured as father in his family for the rest of his life."[5] A man's status, and authority in this case is fully established. "In such marriages the children love and obey their father".[6]

Households with non-heiress wife enjoy considerable degree of independence from the descent groups of both sides. "If a father's activities were such to permit the accumulation of wealth to be handed over to the next generation, he is always remembered in great respect and admiration by his successors and by the descendants of his wife's matrilineal lines. In such a case he is looked upon as a member of his wife's group rather than of his mother's descent group."[7] If he as a father acquires property, this is handed down to his youngest daughter who will bring in her husband on marriage. In this case one may find that the *Khadduh's* family has her father as head of household.

We now can turn to men married to an heiress. In such cases there could be a problem, as it requires a great deal of adjustment for the man. In case the house was acquired by the father of the girl, the husband of the *Khadduh* has to reckon with his father-in-law. If he is a man of means, he is given the due respect by his wife's family, and a total acceptance is ensured. In these cases, the *Khadduh's* brother may find his home and duty usurped by another man and personality clashes may occur. If on the other hand theirs is ancestral property, the uncle and brothers may play a more dominant role.

If the heiress' husband is financially weak as in the cases of early marriages whereby a young boy is forced by circumstances to live in the girl's home as another dependent of her parents, he may have a problem adjusting and receiving the respect of his in-laws. Here, the matrikin of his wife may be the decision-makers. Our data reveal that much depends on the wealth and personality aspects of the husbands.

The role of the father in matrilineal societies is an ambiguous one because the maternal uncle of his children is seen as the figure of authority. This role-perception is highlighted in Table 3 and one finds that the highest percentage of men and women feel that matriliny does not undermine the authority of the father.

Table 4 projects the views on children taking the father's surname: 60% of both male and female respondents are against changing descent patterns. This is for fear of confusion in clan affiliation. Twenty-five per cent of the men and ten per cent of the women are for it, and feel this would solve present social and economic problems of the Khasis. Fifteen per cent of the men and thirty per cent of the women feel that the solution of the problem is by giving both, that is, an indication of the mother's clan should be made along with father's surname.

In traditional Khasi society, the maternal uncle plays a vital role in the lives of his sisters and her children. As is shown in Table 5, 77.5 per cent of male respondents and 80 per cent of female respondents state that the role of the *Kñi* is symbolic, he is now informed of family happenings but he does not make the decisions: 22.5 per cent of the men and 20 per cent of the women feel the maternal uncle plays a decisive role. Most of these respondents who affirmed the

Table 3: Matriliny and Authority of the Father

Does matriliny undermine the authority of the father?	% of Males	% of Females
Yes	35.0	42.5
No	62.5	52.5
To some extent	2.5	5.0
Total	100.0	100.0

Table 4: Views on giving Father's Surname

Views	% of Males	% of Females
Against	60	60
For	25	10
Give both father's name and mother's name	15	30
Total	100.0	100.0

Table 5: Role of the *Kñi*

Role of the *Kñi*	% of Male	% of Females
Symbolic	77.5	80.0
Decisive	22.5	20.0
Total	100.0	100.0

decisive role of the maternal uncles were of the Khasi religion. The role of the maternal uncle or brother is also dependent on residence patterns, property implications and his personality. His role may be more dominant in his natal home, that is, where the *Khadduh* and her family reside.

The Khasi matrilineal system follows the principle of female ultimogeniture in matters of inheritance. By this, it is meant that the youngest daughter called the *Khadduh* or the last surviving daughter has rights to inherit from the mother. Customarily, all daughters, except the youngest, are expected to leave their natal home after marriage to set up independent households. The youngest daughter continues to stay in her natal home with her husband. Two vital issues are brought into focus, firstly there is a constant splitting off of the lineage and each daughter starting her own. Secondly, the continuity of lineage is expressed in terms of mother-youngest daughter units.

The issue of property inheritance has to be discussed in the light of the distinction made between (i) ancestral property or *Nongtymmen* and (ii) self-acquired property or *Nongkhynraw*. As mentioned, the youngest daughter inherits ancestral property; however, this does not imply that other daughters do not receive anything. Depending on the economic capacity of the parents, the others may also receive property of gifts in cash as well as in kind, to help them set up a separate household. Every daughter gets an equal share with the *Khadduh* getting an additional portion to meet all expenses incurred by her for maintenance of property and for other obligations and responsibilities.

As nurturer of the family line, the *Khadduh* has a significant role in the domestic sphere. On her devolves the responsibilities of caring and protecting all members of her matrikin. She is to look after her aged parents and other members of her matrikin if they should suffer from any misfortune. This includes her brothers and sisters who either remain single or divorced. This also includes the children of her sisters. If in case of death of a sister, she becomes responsible for her children. The husband or father is not expected to look after them although he might provide a sum of money for their maintenance. This issue has created problems: on the one hand the *Khadduh* becomes burdened with the responsibility of providing for more members and on the other hand, fathers usually lose contact with their children. Even when no property is inherited, the responsibility of caring and providing for the old parents and other matrikin still falls on the *Khadduh*. She, therefore, has a burden which on many occasions is not shared by other sisters. This is an issue which has been neglected by many and as a result of which, the *Khadduh* has always been portrayed as grabing, spoilt or arrogant.

Table 6 outlines the obligation of the *Khadduh* towards her parents, if she does not inherit any property. In other words, what the role of the *Khadduh* is if there is no inherited property at her disposal. Does she still have the responsibilities of caring for the parents and other matrikin? 77.5 per cent of the male and 75 per cent of the female respondents feel that the *Khadduh* has no obligations. Any of the children who are in a position to take care of the parents should do so. 22.5 per cent of the male and 25 per cent of the female respondents feel that the *Khadduh* has obligation whether there is property or not. Some of the female respondents who also happen to be *Khadduh* feel that the *Khadduh* should not be put under any obligation of looking after parents; but have the right to inherit wealth from the mothers.

A Khasi may say that the gender of a child is not an issue. However, a female child can to a certain extent be considered as old-age security. Present day trends reveal that in case of no female issues, property should go to the son (particularly the youngest) who looks after the parents. Equal provisions to all children regardless of gender is the order of the day. If there is a girl child, she naturally takes up the responsibility

Table 6: Opinion Regarding Obligations of the Khadduh who do not Inherit Property

Obligations of *Khadduh* towards Parents	% of Males	% of Females
No obligation	77.5	75.0
Obligated	22.5	25.0
Total	100.0	100.0

Table 7: Views Regarding Inheritance of Property

Distribution of Property	% of Males	% of Females
Equal among all Children	62.5	95.0
By use of a Will	12.5	0.0
Khadduh should inherit more	25.0	5.0
Total	100.0	100.0

of looking after her parents and inheriting the property. If there is no girl child, any of the sons who are willing to stay with parents inherit. The relevant issue is not who inherits but rather who is willing to take up the responsibility of staying at the ancestral home.

As is shown in Table 7, 62.5 per cent of male respondents and 95 per cent of female respondents feel that property should be equally distributed. Interestingly, the women seemed to favour equal distribution more than the men. Twenty-seven and a half per cent of the men feel that the *Khadduh* should get more than the other children as she looks after the parents. These men seem quite rigid in their outlook, as far as they are concerned the *Khadduh* has her obligations, whether she likes it or not. Just five per cent of the women feel that they should inherit more than the others.

The *Khadduh* may inherit the family property, but plays the role only of a custodian. She, therefore, has to play the roles of perpetuator of the lineage, wife and mother, and daughter to her aged parents. However, as rights imply duties she has an obligation to fulfilling these roles. But it is clear that just as the man she marries has adjustment problems, and tremendous pressures, she too has her share of them. She is constantly torn between loyalties to her matrikin and her husband.

Table 8 shows that 60 per cent of the male respondents and 80 per cent of the female respondents were of the opinion that matriliny is not responsible for marriage disintegration. 27.5 per cent men and 12.5 per cent women agreed that matriliny did play a vital role in the disintegration of marriage, while 7.5 per cent both men and women felt that marriage

Table 8: Matriliny and Disintegration of Marriage

Is matriliny responsible for disintegration of marriage?	% of Males	% of Females
No	65.0	80.0
Yes	27.5	12.5
Because of the *Khadduh*	7.5	7.5
Total	100.0	100.0

with a *Khadduh* was unstable. The break-down of marriages particularly where the *Khadduh* was the wife, can be traced to the interference of the matrikin. It is not the system *per se* which causes disintegration, but rather the rigid interpretation of it.

Influence of kinship ties has to a large extent diminished. As a result of this more importance is attached to the conjugal families. Priority is now given to one's own family members, be it sons or daughters. Social ills particularly the degeneration of the Khasi youth is dominant. Teenage pregnancy, unemployment and violence are on the rise, and the possibility of connecting the three is apparent enough. Incidently, teenage pregnancies have been traced to the matrilineal character of society, the reason being that a child born is integrated into its mother's group. As a result, the social stigma associated with illegitimacy does not exist. However, this does not imply that the society is always tolerant about the unwed-mother. Regardless of popular belief, a certain stigma is attached to a woman known to have several husbands. Society does frown upon such women.

The Khasi mother is also known to be very protective about her male children, owing to the fact that they must leave home, and enter another woman's home. *Khun mih ïng*[8] (or children who have to leave home) and *Khun ki briew* (child of another) are common phrases amongst the Khasis, and these refer to the male child. If the male child cannot cope with his marriage, he has the option of returning home and the duty of caring for him falls on his parents and younger sister. He is, therefore, psychologically geared to "run home" at any provocation. This may sound highly prejudicial; however, these are some of the views reflected by respondents, both male and female. Remedy to this is not in changing the system but by building a sense of responsibility through exposure, education and most importantly employment.

In conclusion, one may say that trends in the way of thinking and acting have definitely undergone a change, but change with caution. Equal opportunities to all children particularly with regard to property distribution are admitted to be necessary. However, tracing descent through the man is rejected. It is believed that the core of Khasi society is its matrilineal character, and if it is changed the culture of the people will disappear. Cultural preservation, therefore, to the Khasi people implies preservation of its matrilineal character. Changes in the urban families are apparent. Influence of kinship ties from the mother has diminished. As a result more importance is attached to conjugal families. In order to achieve a thorough comprehension of those finer details of change, a comparative study between urban and rural settings would be ideal. There is, therefore, scope for further research in those directions.

NOTES AND REFERENCES

1. Reiss, A.J. (ed.), *Louis Wirth on Cities and Social Life: Selected Papers.* Chicago Press, Chicago University, 1964.
2. Rymbai, R.T., *Report of the Land Reforms Commission for Khasi Hills,* Government Press, Meghalaya, Shillong 1974 p. 23.
3. Nakane, C., *Garo and Khasi— a Comparative Study in Matrilineal Systems,* Mouton & Co. Paris, 1967.
4. Syiemlieh, Pynshai Bor, *The Khasis and the Matrilineal System.*
5. Nakane, C., Op. cit., p. 129.
6. Ibid. p. 130.
7. Ibid.
8. *Khun Mih Iing*: This refers not only to the male child but to all children who leave home to start their own households. The phrase, therefore, applies to all children excluding the *Khadduh.*

9

Christian Values Encounter Family in Meghalaya

Dominic Jala

Introduction

If Christianity makes any difference for the societies that it comes across, it is particularly in the values of the family. The Christian perspective regarding the origin of the family focuses on the story of the creation of man and woman. Marriage and family are not the products of purely human or social instincts. There is a transcendental element in the very origin of the family which sustains it and leads it in its transformations. If there is a point of contrast between the Christian perspective and various cultural groups, it is more evident in the area of the unity and indissolubility of marriage. The Catholic view of family anchors itself strongly in these qualities of marriage. Monogamy and the inadmissibility of divorce have brought the church and the world into positions of conflicting contrasts. The upholding of these two is seen as indispensable for the integrity of the family. The language of Christian theology has become more personalistic in this area. Earlier Christians spoke of the contract of marriage. Today, we speak of a "covenant-relationship" in marriage, resembling the solemn agreement God himself made with people. In the earlier Christian manuals, marriage used to be described in terms of begetting children. The language has changed, providing us also with a broader and richer view of the meaning of family: the service of life, life of the newly conceived person, the lives of the married couple, and the lives of the children, extending further to life beyond the family unit itself.

Family integrity and the attaining of its finality will not be assured unless there is respect for the dignity of every person. The modern issues on the dignity of the woman in the family setting, the rights of the child, the right to work, the right to a just wage and other such rights and related duties cannot be understood apart from a correct view of the human person.

The Meghalayan Family in Transition

It may be difficult to describe the Meghalayan family situation today, but we cannot deny that it has undergone enormous changes during the past century, since the societies of present day Meghalaya came into contact with Christianity. Social scientists may be able to indicate more clearly the factors that underlie the changes that have taken place. As an amateur, I may indicate some of the not so strictly religious factors which, however, have also come along with, if not exclusively on account of, the advent of Christianity.

There has been a rapid transformation of the family pattern from the traditional one. The nuclear type of family structure is now becoming more prevalent. More and more, the family today is not confined to a village set-up where the newly married couples live in the vicinity to the original parental family. One of the reasons for this is the changed economic structure of Meghalayan society today. Though agriculture remains the mainstay of the majority of the people, alternative means for earning a living away from the home village have brought about a new situation which has also affected the family. Another factor linked to the changing economy is the urbanization process. Migrant families are on the increase in the major towns of the state. This makes it difficult for traditional contacts between related families. Independence of each family unit is the result.

Education which took a formal turn with the coming of British rule and which was developed by the various missionary groups, whether Christian or not, has also transformed the traditional Meghalayan family. The farming based family, having educated children, gradually gets weaned away from a purely agro-based dependence. The new generation may also move away from agriculture in pursuit of other less burdensome, less risky and more rewarding kinds of enterprises. This at times, can tell heavily on the resources of the family.

One of the current debated issues in Khasi society in the state of Meghalaya, is the move to change over from matriliny to patriliny. *The Seng Rympei Thymmai* (SRT) is trying its level best to initiate changes within its fold and to introduce changes in society. A number of sensitive issues are linked to the move. What is to become of traditional system of the *Khasi Khein kur?* How is exogamous marriage to be assured ? Will this solve the problem of male irresponsibility ? Will it cure the socio-economic ills that numerous seminars and discussions have pointed out as afflicting Khasi society ? The Garo society has not come forward with any such revolutionary schemes.

The availability of better health care also affects the family today. The risk of infant mortality is drastically reduced. The average life expectancy has gone up. Young people today, especially if educated, may tend to marry at a later age. In older agricultural societies, early marriages were the norm. The period of youth increases, making the family pattern itself different with members of the family staying together for a longer period of time.

Together with the above changes in current Meghalayan society, the decadence of traditional family values is often bemoaned. Single parent families (usually supported by the single mother) are becoming more and more common. The phenomenon cuts through all kinds of religious affiliations and causes concern to all those involved in ministering to society.

How far is Christianity responsible for the changes that have taken place ? This is not an easy question to answer. Social scientists may be able to indicate some lines of reference here. The question may appear strongly academic but it can provide guiding lights for the future course of action.

What has Christianity to Offer

The Christian Churches cannot absolve themselves of their responsibility towards the family. The Christian insistence on the "sacredness" of the family is a challenge to the present day trend of commercialising family life. When consumerism begins to engulf the family, priorities other than the deeply human ones begin to emerge. Christianity has brought to our society a view that the family relationship is something deeper than purely social bond. The dignity of the human person has been strongly insisted upon in Church teaching. The dignity of the woman, as life-partner and, as mother is a repeated theme in Christian teaching. The struggle in Khasi society today to strengthen the position of the man in the family and to foster the care for and the equal rights of the boy child is based on the awareness of the basic equal dignity of the human person, whether boy or girl, man or woman. The lack of this awareness on the part of the boy-man as well as on the part of the leaders of the family also lies at the root of the lack of a sense of direction in male society of Meghalaya.

However, we note that Christianity as such, while originating in a patriarchal culture, never sought to destroy the matrilineal culture of the Khasi or Garo people. At the same time, the call of Christianity to respect the equal dignity of every person, challenges any society where injustice or under-privileged situations may prevail. The present questions placed before matrilineal society may not be direct offshoot of Christian teaching, but we can still search for the relationship between the Christian world view and the dissatisfaction with social organization. Christianity as such will not provide an answer as to whether matriliny or patriliny is to be preferred but it questions any system where the rights and the dignity of a person are not respected.

The Church, particularly the Catholic Church, stands for stability in marriage, which is the foundation of family life. The trauma engulfing broken families speaks enough for the problems in society where stability is not assured. In a world where the media and current trends tend to trivialize the strong bond of the family hearth, there is the need of a strong voice challenging the ways in which many may still prefer to go.

10

Status of Garo Women in the Nineteenth Century

Frederick S. Downs

The value of work done by historians is in large measure determined by the quality of the sources they use. Consequently, one of the most important aspects of historians' work is the evaluation of those sources. There was a school of positive historians who used to say that "the facts speak for themselves." All one needed to do was collect the "facts" as they are presented in sources and certain conclusions would necessarily follow. Historians were primarily in the business of searching for and finding "facts" in a variety of different sources. We have since learned that it is not as simple as that. Sources do not "speak for themselves". They have to be evaluated and interpreted by the historian. After finishing this process, it is historians who speak on the basis of their evaluation of the data, not the sources themselves. In other words, historians are trying to determine, on the basis of accepted evaluative procedures, just what the "facts" are to which the sources seem to point.

This essay seeks to show how difficult this task can be for the historian — and at the same time introduce material that is of sociological interest. While I was doing research for an essay on Ms. Miriam Russell, I came across an extraordinary letter in the archives of the Board of International Ministries, American Baptist Churches. This was a letter[1] that had been written to the Woman's Baptist Missionary Society[2] by the annual meeting of the Garo Association (*Krima*), meeting at Tura in 1897. It reads as follows:

> To the Society of Beloved Mothers in America, is this letter written. Before you, in love to us, sent us "lady missionaries", how much the Garo women spent their time in doing deeds of darkness that we cannot tell. According to our family laws the woman is master of the riches of the house; therefore, they magnified themselves, were proud, despised their husbands, were not in subjection to them, taught evil to their daughters, and all went astray. But when, by the leading hand of God, you in love sent with the missionaries "lady teachers", viz., Miss Russell, Miss Mason, Miss Bond, and then Miss Rood, to show them what they were needing to learn, and thus starting the school for girls at Tura, gathering them together there, and with God's guidance zealously teaching them to read, to sew and to knit, because of this, the Garo women are now learning to read books, the Scriptures, to sew, and not these alone, for although they are not yet perfect they are better than before. They teach their children better, look after their houses and granaries better, love and honor their husbands more. Therefore, we thank God. We, the brothers, mothers, sisters of the churches of the Krima Association, seeing your loving help to us for the good of the Garo women, rejoice. We send you our greeting.[3]

If this letter "speaks for itself", one would have to conclude that prior to the coming of missionaries of the WBMS, Garo women were not only illiterate and incapable of properly managing the affairs of their households, but that they were a "proud" lot who regarded themselves as superior to their husbands because they were the inheritors of the ancestral property. One can only imagine what the "deeds of darkness" to which they devoted so much time were. Only after the coming of Christianity did they learn to "love and honor their husbands more." This letter seems to speak of a time when matriliny was practised within a matriarchal society.

There are very few documents from the nineteenth century which provide us with information about the status of women among the Garos at that time. There is, however, another source that calls into question the assumption that because Garo women traditionally inherited the family property they, "magnified themselves, were proud, despised their husbands, were not in subjection to them, taught evil to their daughters, and all went astray." This was a paper[4] read at the Jubilee Conference of the American Baptist Mission held in Nagaon in 1886 by Miriam Russell, one of the women mentioned in the Krima letter of 1897. She served in the Garo Hills from 1879 till 1884, some thirteen years prior to the writing of the Krima letter. The jubilee conference paper was about Garo women. Reflecting on the time she spent with Garo women in North side villages during two winter seasons, she thus describes their status in relationship to men:

> Unlike women of the plains, they (Garo women) appear to enjoy perfect freedom. They attend religious services, go to the weekly market, visiting neighbouring villages and, in company with male relatives, often visit distant places. When speaking of a man and wife, the woman's name is mentioned first; this would seem to show respect to her, . . . The Garos say that the man and not the woman would be offended by inverting the expression. Owing to the fact that property descends through the female instead of the male line (the Garo social structure is matrilineal), the women seem to have great honor. A more intimate acquaintance with the people, however, shows that the women are not honored by the men but are really held in contempt by them. A man may cruelly beat his wife, but if she so much as strike him once, he can cast her off. It degrades a man to have a woman sit in front of him. She must not eat before her husband has been helped. . . The freedom of the Garo woman differs from that of the Purdah-woman of the plains in kind rather than in degree. In both cases, the word of the man is the law that governs her actions.[5]

"Speaking for itself" this document indicates that the Garo society of the late nineteenth century while matrilineal was very clearly patriarchal. Women were roughly and unequally treated by their husbands, and not honoured by men, who completely controlled their lives.

In other words the paper presents an entirely different view from the letter. Which is correct? Historians obviously cannot accept each at face value. They must carry out a process of evaluation based upon context analysis. Two primary elements in the context in this case are authorship and purpose.

Authorship of the Paper

The authorship of the paper is clear. Miriam Russell, as indicated above, served as the first missionary of the WBMS among the Garos. She was stationed in Tura for five years between 1879 and 1884. After that she married and moved to Guwahati. In Guwahati she had contact with plains Garos in Kamrup. With only seven years' experience with the Garos, how much weight can be given to Russell's observations? Especially when compared to the letter which was purportedly written by Garos? Normally one would give greater weightage to the latter. But Russell's remarks were based upon a more intimate and prolonged experience of Garo society than was usual among missionaries of that time. They were not based upon observations made in Tura where the Christian community was under the dominating influence of the missionaries, but in Garo villages. Early in 1882 she spent seven weeks touring along a route on which she visited fifteen villages between Tura and the north side. During two of those weeks she was accompanied by a Christian school boy, but otherwise she was on her own among Songsarik Garos — at least until she reached the north side at the end of her tour where she was joined by the other Tura missionaries attending the annual Krima being held in the area. Almost two years later, during the winter season of 1883-84, she spent two months running a model village school in Nisangram on the north side. She lived simply in a Garo house and could communicate only through the Garo language. As she put it, "living in the native village gave me an opportunity that I could have gained in no other way of becoming acquainted with the every day lives of the Christian women."[6]

This brings us to the authorship of the letter. It is purported to have been written to the WBMS by the Garo

Christians, women and men, gathered in Tura for the annual Krima in 1897. I say "purported" because it is in English, a language in which no Garos of that time would have been sufficiently proficient to produce the letter in the form we have it. At the very least it would have been translated by a missionary. By definition this makes it a secondary rather than a primary source. Translation always involves a measure of interpretation. Furthermore, *Krimas* of those days were dominated by the Tura missionaries. No business could have been transacted except at the suggestion or with the approval of those missionaries. It is also worth noting that the mission organization of those days was highly patriarchal. In its affairs the women missionaries — either wives or unmarried women — had little say, except in matters concerning their particular sphere of work. It is highly unlikely that the letter was the work of Garos without male missionary influence and interpretation.

Purpose of the Paper

The relative value of the paper written in 1886 by a woman missionary and the missionary-translated letter sent to the WBMS by the Krima in 1897 can perhaps be determined by an assessment of the purposes behind each. While not a feminist in the modern sense, Russell was a representative of the WBMS, an organization that had been created precisely because American Baptist women did not trust the men of the general society (then known as the American Baptist Missionary Union)[7] to carry out their agenda on behalf of women in the countries to which missionaries went.[8] The WBMS was a part of the woman's movement that was dedicated to securing for women rights equal to those enjoyed by men in such areas as inheritance, custody of children, divorce, education and voting. Its mission was to similarly liberate its sisters in Asia and Africa from societies that oppressed them. The working assumption was that women were oppressed by men in all societies. The injustices of female foot-binding in China and the Zenana system in India were obvious. Less obvious was the subordination and oppression of women in the matrilineal Garo society.[9] It could be argued, therefore, that Russell was looking for some justification for the work of the WBMS among Garo women — and that this influenced her perception of the situation.

The purposes of the letter are more complex. On the surface of it, the letter was sent to thank the WBMS for sending women missionaries to work on behalf of Garo girls and women. It can be inferred that it was also a request that such missionaries should continue to be sent among them. Both Garo Christians and missionaries would have endorsed this purpose. But the letter seems to have a larger aim. That was to justify the conversion of the Garos to Christianity. Hence a familiar form of missiological analysis is introduced: previously the Garos lived in darkness, now they live in light. In this particular letter the familiar theme is applied to the condition of women or, more precisely, the relationship between women and men. The determination of what constitutes darkness and what constitutes light in those relationships is clearly based on patriarchal assumptions. A situation in which women "magnified themselves, were proud, despised their husbands, were not in subjection to them, taught evil to their daughters, and all went astray" is darkness. Matriarchy is by definition darkness.[10] Light, and patriarchy, comes with Christianity. There is now a higher social order among Garo Christians, one in which wives are duly submissive to and honour their husbands. This underlying missiological purpose may have been directed as much to Garo women as to the "beloved mothers" in America.

Evaluation

How are historians to evaluate these sources in the light of their authorship and purpose? Was traditional Garo society essentially matriarchal, as the letter would suggest, or was it patriarchal as the paper asserts? Were women traditionally entirely free of male dominance, or were they subordinate to men?

If the letter had been written and translated by Garos without any missionary influence, we would have to give it more credence. After all, it would then represent Garos description of their own society and the historical experience of the impact of Christianity with respect to the relationship between women and men. For the reasons that have been given, this is highly improbable. Missionary influence upon any action of the Krima was strong and, in any event, the letter was almost certainly translated by a missionary. Furthermore, it was missionaries who decided to forward it to the WBMS.

The earlier paper was transparently the work of a missionary, a missionary with some experience of the actual realities of Garo society at the village level. However, the village in which she had the most extensive exposure to that society was Nisangram, one of the first Garo villages in which a Christian community had been established. Her experience there was therefore of a society already under Christian (patriarchal?) influence. How much change would have been brought about in fundamental attitudes in the few years a Christian community had existed there? Nisangram had not had the "benefit" of a regular missionary presence, hence missionary influence would have been minimal. A full evaluation of the situation would involve an attempt to determine how much Ramke, the most influential Garo Christian leader in the area, had been influenced by the patriarchy of the Assamese society in which he had lived for a number of years. But that is beyond the scope of this essay. We have also suggested that Russell was not entirely objective observer. She was a woman predisposed by her association with the WBMS to look for evidence of the oppression of females.

The purposes of the paper are more transparent than those of the letter. The author is seeking to improve the condition of women, a social agenda which she believes is implied in the Gospel. While the letter is an expression of thanks, it also has a missiological agenda which seeks to contrast previous "darkness" with present "light". Under the influence of a patriarchal perspective it presupposes that a situation in which women are not controlled by men is "darkness", and one in which they are duly submissive to men is "light".

The apparent influence of a missionary patriarchal ideology on the letter, an influence which probably leads to considerable exaggeration of the matriarchal tendencies in traditional Garo society, makes it less credible as a source. Another aspect of the evaluative procedures followed by historians that has not thus far been mentioned also tends to support the conclusion that Russell's letter is a more credible description of the relationship between women and men in traditional Garo society than the Krima letter — that is, corroboration. While there are not many sources dealing with this subject from a period as early as those we have considered here, the substantial anthropological studies that had begun to be made by the early twentieth century tend to support the conclusions reached in the paper rather than those of the letter. Uninformed descriptions of Meghalaya as the "land where women rule" notwithstanding, virtually all anthropologists have described traditional Garo society as matriliny within a patriarchal structure. While the female lineage determines inheritance of ancestral property (by the youngest daughter normally) and clan and sub-clan identity, governance and therefore real power was in the hands of males. They also concur with Russell's view that however much importance was given to a female child, men dominated and in numerous practical ways were treated as superior to women. The fact that scholars agree does not necessarily make them right. If we could be sure that the letter was written by Garos without missionary influence, and without the need to find justification for their own conversion to Christianity, it would have to be taken very seriously as a primary source.

Because this historian believes that the letter is seriously compromised in both its authorship and purpose, he concludes that Russell's paper, which corroborates later studies of Garo society, has to be given more credence.

NOTES AND REFERENCES

1. Hereafter referred to simply as "the letter".
2. From 1871 until the early 1950s the American Baptist Churches had two mission societies — one for men and their wives, and the other exclusively for unmarried women. The women's society was first called the Woman's Baptist Missionary Society (WBMS) and, later, the Women's American Baptist Foreign Mission Society (WABFMS).
3. 1898 Annual Report of the Woman's Baptist Missionary Society.
4. Hereafter referred to simply as "the paper".

5. *The Assam Mission of the American Baptist Missionary Union. Papers and Discussion of the Jubilee Conference held in Nowgong, December 18–29, 1886*, (Gauhati: ABMU Assam Mission, 1887), p. 198. See also Frederick S. Downs, "Miriam Russell Burdette," *American Baptist Quarterly*, XII 3 (September 1993), pp. 242–8.
6. *Jubilee Conference, 1886*, p. 198.
7. Later the name was changed to the American Baptist Foreign Mission Society (ABFMS) and eventually to the Board of International Ministries, American Baptist Churches (BIM). Among American Baptists the BIM is known simply as International Ministries.
8. I discuss the context within which the women's missionary societies were established in the west in my H.K. Barpujari Endowment Lectures, NEHU, 1994.
9. It is interesting that though an important part of the nineteenth century Woman's Movement in the United States was the demand that daughter should have equal inheritance rights with sons, I have seen no evidence of any missionary, male or female, questioning the inequities of an inheritance system in which only one daughter and no son may inherit! The policy of the American Baptist Mission, like that of other missionary societies of the time, was to accept all traditional social practices so long as they had no religious significance in the old order.
10. This provides an interesting contrast with the view of Frederich Engels that matriarchy is the original and pure state of human social organization.

Select Bibliography

Pariyaram M. Chacko

Badwar, Magdeline, 1987. 'Some Institutional Factors Retarding Economic Progress Among the Khasi Community', (Mimeo) Paper presented in Seminar: Institutional Economics and the North-Eastern Region's Economy, Shillong: Deptt. of Economics, NEHU.

Bareh, Hamlet, 1974. *Meghalaya* Shillong: North Eastern India News and Feature Service.

Barkataki, S., 1969. *The Tribes of Assam*, New Delhi: National Book Trust of India.

Bhandari, J.S. (ed), 1996. *Kinship and Family in the North-East,* New Delhi: Cosmo Publications.

Bhat, Sudhakar, 1975. *The Challenge of the North East* Bombay: Popular Prakashan.

Bhattacharjee, J.B., 1984. 'Changing Khasis A Historical Account' in S. Karotemporel (ed) *The Tribes of North-Eastern India,* Shillong: Vendrame Missiological Institute, pp. 319–335.

Bhattacharjee, J.B. (ed.), 1989. *Sequences of Development in North East India*, New Delhi: Omsons.

Burling Robins, 1958. "Garo Avuncncular Authority and Matrilineal Cross-Cousin Marriage", *American Anthropologist,* No. 4. pp. 743–749.

Burling, Robins, 1963. *Rengsangiri (Family and Kinship in a Garo Village),* Philadelphia: University of Pennsylvania Press.

Cantlie Keith, 1974. *Notes on Khasi Law*, edited and reprinted by; A.S. Khongphai, Shillong: Ri Khasi Press (First Published 1934).

Choudhury, Bhupendranath, 1958. *Some Cultural and Linguistic Aspects of the Garos,* Gauhati: Lawyers Book Stall.

Choudhury, J.N., 1978. *The Khasi Canvas: A Cultural and Political Hisstory* Shillong: Chapala Book Stall.

Chattopadhyaya, S.K. (ed), 1985. *Tribal Institutions of Meghalaya,* Guwahati: Spectrum Publications.

Chattopadhayaya, S.K., 1988. *The Jaintias,* New Delhi: Cosmo.

Chattopadhyay, K.P., 1948 "Khasi Land Ownership and Sale", *Eastern Anthropologist,* Vol. 2, pp. 133–137.

Chattopadhyay, K.P., 1941. *"Khasi Kinship and Social Organisation" University of Calcutta, Anthropological Papers,* New Series, No. 6 p. 1–39.

Chib, S.S., 1984. *Caste, Tribes, and Culture of India,* Vol. 8. *North-Eastern India,* New Delhi: ESS Publications.

Dalton, E.T., 1973. Tribal History of Eastern India, Delhi: Cosmo. [Original title: Descriptive Ethnology of Bengla, 1872, Calcutta: Govt. Press].

Das, N.K., 1982. "Review of the Works on Social Structures of Some Matrilineal Tribes of North-East India and Observations Theron", *Journal of the Indian Anthropological Society,* 17, pp. 199–214.

Dasgupta, P.K., 1961. "Riseng or Land of Cognates Among the War Khasi", *Eastern Anthropologist,* vol. 14, No. 2.

Dasgupta, P.K., 1964. "Marriage Among the War Khasi", *Man in India.* Vol. 44, No. 2, pp. 146–160.

Dasgupta, P.K., 1984. *Life and Culture of Matrilineal Tribe of Meghalaya,* New Delhi: Inter India.

Deb Roy, H.L., 1981. *A Tribe in Transition: The Jaintias of Meghalaya:* New Delhi: Cosmo.

Dutta, Promotha Nath, 1982. *Impact of the West on the Khasis and Jaintias: A Survey of Political Economic and social Change,* New Delhi: Cosmo.

Downs, Frederick, S. 1992. *History of Christianity in India,* Vol. V. Part 5, *North-East India in the Nineteenth Centuries,* Bangalore. The Church History Association, India.

Ehrenfels, U.R.,1953. "Khasi Kinship Term in Four Dialects", *Anthropos,* Vol. 48, Nos. 3 & 4, pp. 396–412.

Ehrenfels, U.R., 1955. "Three Matrilineal Groups of Assam" *American Anthropologist,* Vol. 57, No. 2. Part. I. pp. 306–321.

Gemini, Paul, 1956. "The Place of Khadduh — The Youngest Daughter in Khasi and Synteng Society", *Vanyajati* Vol. 4. pp. 82–84.

George, M.C. (ed), 1990. *Centenary of the Catholic Church in North-East India 1890–1990: A Souvenir,* Shillong: Archbishop's House.

Giri, Helen, 1990. *Khasi Under British Rule (1842–1947)* Shillong: Akashi Book Depot.

Goswami B.B. (ed), 1979. *Cultural Profile of Shillong,* Calcutta: Anthropological Survey of India.

Gurdon, P.R.T., 1987. *The Khasis,* (reprint) New Delhi: Cosmo. (First Published by Govt. of Eastern Bengal and Assam 1907).

Gurdon, P.R.T., 1904. "Note on the Khasis, Syntengs and Allied Tribes Inhabiting the Khasi and Jaintia Hills District of Assam", *Journal of the Asiatic Society of Bengal,* Vol. 73, part 3. pp. 57–74.

Hodson, T.C., 1921. "The Garo and Khasi Marriage Systems Contrasted", *Man in India,* Vol. I. pp. 106–127.

Indian Anthropological Society, 1978. *Tribal Women in India,* Calcutta.

Indian Law Institute, 1982. *Customary Law and Justice in Tribal Areas of Meghalaya,* Bombay: N.M. Tripathi Ltd.

Kanwar, H.I.S., *"The Khasia; Nature's Own Offspring", Indian Geographer'* Vol. I. pp. 88–92.

Rat, Parimal Chandra, 1982. *Garos in Transition,* New Delhi: Cosmo.

Karotemprel, S. (ed), *The Tribes of North-East India,* Shillong: Vendrame Misiological Institute.

Karotemprel, S. (ed), 1993. *The Catholic Church in North-East India 1890-1990,* Shillong: Vendrame Institute.

Khongsdier, R., 1996. "A Note on Micro-Social Variation in the War Khasi with Speicial Reference to Inheritance Property" *Journal of North-East Council for Social Science Research,* Vol. 20. No. 2.

Majumdar, D.N., 1956. *The Garos* Gauhati: The Lawyers' Book Stall.

Majumdar, D.N., 1980. *A Study of the Culture Change in Two Garo Villages of Meghalaya,* Calcutta: The Pooram Press.

Majumdar, D.N., and M.C. Goswami, 1973. *Social Institutions of the Garos of Meghalaya,* Calcutta.

Marak, J.L.R., 1985. *Garo Customary Laws and Practices,* Shillong: Vendrame Missiological Institute.

Mathew, T. (ed), 1980. *Tribal Economy of North Eastern Region,* Gauhati: Spectrum.

Mathur, P.R.G., 1979. *The Khasi of Meghalaya: A Study in Tribalism and Religion,* New Delhi: Cosmo.

Mawlong, Aldila M .,1996. Aspects of Change in the Family System Among the Khasis, M.Phil. Dissertation, Shillong, Deptt. of Sociology, North-Eastern Hill University, 1996.

Mawrie, H.O., 1981. *The Khasi Milieu,* New Delhi: Concept.

Mills, A.J.M., 1853. *Report on the Khasi, Jaintia Hills,* Reprinted by North-Eastern Hill University, Shillong: 1985.

Minattur, Joseph, 1955. "The Khasis", *Modern Review,* Vol. 97. pp. 389–395.

Miri, Sujata, 1988. *Khasi World View: A Conceptual Exploration,* Chandigarh: Centre for Research in Rural and Industrial Development.

Mukherjee, Bhabananda, 1958. "Social Groupings Among the Khasis of Assam, *Man in India,* Vol. 38, No. 3. pp. 208–212.

Mukherjee, S. et. al. (eds), 1994. *Demographic Profile of North East India,* New Delhi: Omsons Publications.

Mukhim, Patricia, 1996. 'Distortions in Our Text Books', *Shillong Times,* April 19.

Nakane, Chie, 1967. *Garo and Khasi: A Comparative Study in Matrilineal System,* Paris: Mouton & Co. The Hague.

Nakane, Chie, "Changes of Matrilineal Families in Assam", Translations of the Third World Congress of Sosciology, Vol. 4. pp. 231–235.

Natarajan, Nalini, 1977. *The Missionary Among the Khasis,* New Delhi: Sterling.

Nongbri, Tiplut, 1984. "Problem of Matriliny: A Short Review of Khasi Kinship Structure", *Journal of North East India Council for Social Science Research,* 8, pp. 1–10.

Nongbri, Tiplut, 1988. "Gender and the Khasi Family Structure: Some Implications of the Meghalaya Succession Act, 1984", *Sociological Bulletin,* 37(1&2) pp. 71–82.

Nongbri, Tiplut, 1995. "Tribal Women and the Family in the Context of Meghalaya" (Mimeo) Paper Presented in a Seminar on Changing Aspects of Family in Meghalaya, Shilong: Deptt. of Sociology, NEHU.

Nonykynrih, A.K., 1990. "Kinship and the Dynamics of Inheritance: A Sociological Study of Matriliny", M.Phil. Dissertation, Shilong, Deptt. of Sociology, NEHU.

Rymbai, R. Tokim, 1974. *Report of the Land Reforms Commission for Khasi Hills,* Shillong: Govt. of Meghalaya.

Pakem, B. (ed), 1984. *Shillong 1971–1981,* Calcutta: Research India Publications.

Pakem, B., 1994. "Socio-legal Status of Women under Matrilineal Society of North-East India" and "Matriliny in 21st Century India" (Mimeo), Lectures delivered at Gauhati Government Law College Guwahati, 28th May.

Passah, P.M., 1988. "Inheritance Among Matrilineal Tribes of North Eastern Region of India: Its Socio-Economic Implications and Evolution", *Vision* Vol. 7, Nos. 3 & 4, pp. 34–41.

Playfair, Major A., 1975. *The Garos,* Gauhati: United Publishers (Reprint) First Published 1909.

Poonthuruthil, James, 1993. 'The Christian Impact on Khasi Family' in S. Karotemprel (ed) *The Catholic Church in North-East India 1890–1990,* Shillong: Vendrame Institute, pp. 438–451.

Roy B. Datta, 1986. *The Pattern and Problems of Population in North-Easst India,* New Delhi: Uppal.

Roy, David, 1936. "Principles of Khasi Culture", *Folk-Lore,* Vol. 47. pp. 375–393.

Roy, Sarat Chandra, 1921. "Khasi Kinship Terms", *Man in India* Vol. 1 pp. 233–238.

Sangma, Milton, S., 1979. *History and Culture of the Garos,* New Delhi: Books Today.

Schneider, David and Kathleen, Gough (eds), 1961. *Matrilineal Kinship,* Berkeley: University of California Press.

Sen, Sipra, 1985. *The Tribes of Meghalaya,* Delhi: Mittal.

Sen, Soumen, (ed), 1992. *Women in Meghalaya,* Daya Publishing House.

Sen, Soumen, (ed), 1993. *Religion in North East India,* New Delhi: Uppal.

Shadap, Sen Namkita, 1981. *Origin and Early History of the Khasi-synteng People,* Calcutta: Firma KLM.

Simon, I.M., 1966. *Khasi and Jaintia Tales and Beliefs,* Gauhati: Deptt. of Tribal Culture and Folklore Research, Gauhati University.

Singh K.S., (ed), 1994. *People of India: Meghalaya,* Vol. XXXII, Calcutta: Seagull Books.

Sinha, A.P., 1986. *Changing North-East India,* Ludhiana: Gagan Publishers.

Sinha A.P., 1985. 'The Pnar Family' in Chattopadhyay (ed) *Tribal in-stitutions of Meghalaya,* Gauhati: Spectrum Publications, pp. 195–210.

Sinha, A.P., 1974. 'Status-Role of the Matrilineal Pnar Husband' in K.S. Mathur and B.C. Agarwal (eds.), *Tribe, Caste and Peasantry,* Lucknow: Ethnographic and Folk Culture Society.

Sinha, Kamleswerl, 1970. *Meghalaya, Triumph of the Tribal Genius,* New Delhi: Publication Division (I.S.S.D.)

Strickland-Anderson, Lily, 1924. "Some Notes on the Customs of Khasi People of Assam", *Journal of the Asiatic Society of Bengal,* Vol. 20. pp. 263-276.

Syiemlieh, David R., 1989. *British Administrtion in Meghalaya, Policy and Pattern,* New Delhi: Heritage.

Syiemlieh, Pynshai Bor, 1994. *The Khasis and Their Matrilineal System,* (A pamphlet) Shillong.

Synrem, H.K., 1992. *Revivalism in Khasi Society* New Delhi: Sterling.

Uberoi, Patricia, (ed), 1993. *Family and Kinship and Marriage In India,* Delhi: Oxford University Press.

Vincent, Kaushal, 1978. *Socio-Economic Study of Bhoilymbong: A Village in Meghalaya,* Madras: Christian Literature Society.

Yule, H. "Notes on the Khasi Hills and People", *Journal of the Asiatic Society of Bengal* Vol. 13, Part. 2. pp. 612–631.

Index